THE BIBLE STORY

VOLUME VI

STRUGGLES AND VICTORIES

(From Daniel to Malachi)

The
BIBLE STORY

More Than Four Hundred Stories in Ten Volumes
Covering the Entire Bible From Genesis to Revelation

VOLUME SIX
Struggles and Victories

BY ARTHUR S. MAXWELL

Author of *Uncle Arthur's Bedtime Stories, The Children's Hour With Uncle Arthur,
The Secret of the Cave*, etc.

PACIFIC PRESS PUBLISHING ASSOCIATION
Mountain View, California

CONTENTS

Part I—Stories of Daniel

Part II—Stories of Israel's Return

— PAINTING BY RUSSELL HARLAN   © 1955, BY REVIEW AND HERALD

Daniel and his three companions were chosen
by Nebuchadnezzar from among the many captives taken from Jerusalem, to be educated in
the schools of Babylon as leaders of the nation.

Part III—Stories of Queen Esther

ESTHER 1:1-10:3

Part IV—Stories of Famous Men

JOB, JONAH, JOEL, MALACHI

PART I

Stories of Daniel

(DANIEL 1:1-12:13)

STORY 1

Four Noble Boys

"WHERE am I?" asked Daniel, rubbing his eyes. "Prison!" muttered Hananiah, who lay beside him in the dungeon. "We're in Babylon."

Babylon! Suddenly it all came back. Those last terrible days in Jerusalem; the long siege, with its hunger, fear, and despair; the breaking down of the city gates; the final onrush of the fierce Babylonian soldiers; the dead bodies of friends and loved ones; the screaming women; the frightened children.

What a nightmare! Daniel remembered how the prisoners had been seized and bound, the dreadful march across the desert to Babylon, the blows and curses of the conquerors, and finally prison.

Now, as the morning sun shone through the grating above their heads, Daniel, Hananiah, Mishael, and Azariah began to realize what a sad, sad thing had happened to them. All four belonged to good families in Judah. From childhood they had enjoyed the best of everything. Now they had nothing, not even freedom.

9

Daniel and his companions purposed in their hearts not to be defiled with the dainties and wine offered to them from the king's table, and asked to be served only the plainest food.

As they looked ahead the future seemed dark indeed. Never again would they see their beloved country, nor their homes, their fathers and mothers, their brothers and sisters. All were gone forever. For the rest of their lives they would be slaves of a hated enemy.

As they talked together they must have asked each other, Why did it all happen? Then they remembered the warnings of Jeremiah that just such punishments would come if the people did not give up their idols and turn again to God. Perhaps right there in prison the four young men asked God's forgiveness for their sins and made up their minds to be true to Him always, no matter what the Babylonians might do to them.

One day the prison door opened, and an officer named Ashpenaz came in. He looked over the prisoners and picked out Daniel, Hananiah, Mishael, and Azariah. At first they wondered why. Had they done something wrong?

Then Ashpenaz explained that Nebuchadnezzar was a great and farseeing king. He did not kill all his captives. Instead he chose the best of them, those who appeared strong,

10

healthy, and intelligent, and educated them in the schools of Babylon so that they might become a strength to the country in days to come. The four boys, he said, should consider themselves very fortunate that they were among the few chosen for this honor.

They did. They were happy indeed. But they were worried as to what it might mean. Would they be expected to worship the gods of Babylon? Would they have to take part in the worship of heathen idols?

Their worries grew when Ashpenaz told them that their names would be changed. Henceforth they would have Babylonian, not Hebrew, names. Daniel was given the name of Belteshazzar; Hananiah was called Shadrach; Mishael, Meshach; and Azariah, Abednego.

From this it seemed clear that their masters meant to change them completely. They were to forget they were Hebrews and become part and parcel of Babylon.

Then came the first big test.

King Nebuchadnezzar gave orders that the captives who had been chosen to be taught "the learning and the tongue of the Chaldeans" should be fed from the king's table. In other words, they were to eat what he ate.

No doubt the king thought he was doing the captives a very great favor in providing them a portion "of the king's meat, and of the wine which he drank"—and he was. But Daniel and his friends were troubled. They felt they couldn't eat the meat that was prepared for the king. For one thing it was probably first offered to idols. For another, much of it no doubt was pig's flesh, or pork, forbidden by God as one of the "unclean" foods. As for the wine, it was fermented, and full of alcohol, so they couldn't take that anyway.

What to do? Was it worth fussing about? After all, it was only food and drink. Maybe they could take just a little and so avoid offending the king. Surely when a heathen king had gone so far in trying to be kind and generous to his captives it would be downright rude not to take the food and drink he gave them.

"But Daniel purposed in his heart that he would not defile himself with the portion of the king's meat, nor with the wine which he drank."

He felt that if he were to yield on this point he would give away everything. He could never take a stand on anything else. If he was going to be loyal to God all the way, he had better start here and now.

So Daniel plucked up his courage and spoke to Ashpenaz. Most respectfully he explained why he and his three friends could not take the food so kindly offered them; would it be all right if they had something else? Nothing special of course; just vegetables and cereals, and good plain water to drink.

Ashpenaz listened patiently. He liked this young man. Indeed "God had brought Daniel into favour and tender love" with him. But now he was worried. He didn't see how it could be done.

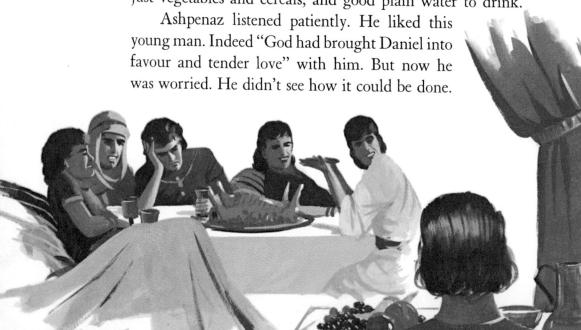

"I fear my lord the king," he said. "If you don't eat the food he has provided, and you become thinner than the rest of the boys, he'll take my head off."

Daniel knew how easily this could happen. Yet he felt sure all would be well. So he went to Melzar, whom Ashpenaz had put in charge of the four, and told him what they wanted to do. "Just let us try it for ten days," he pleaded. "Give us pulse to eat, and water to drink. Then look us over and do what seems best."

With many misgivings Melzar agreed. Instead of the king's meat and wine he gave them vegetables, cereals, and water. And you can imagine how he watched them day by day for the first signs of weakness!

But they didn't fall sick as Melzar expected. Nor did their faces grow thin and pale. Instead, "at the end of ten days their countenances appeared fairer and fatter in flesh than all the children which did eat the portion of the king's meat."

Melzar was surprised and very pleased. From now on he gladly gave the four boys the food they wanted. And somehow they were able to think more clearly than the others. They

remembered their lessons better. Living on a clean, simple diet, they were able to gather knowledge and wisdom faster than all the rest put together.

At the end of three years they were graduated from school with highest honors. As a special reward they were presented to King Nebuchadnezzar. "And the king communed with them."

They had never expected this! Certainly not on that far-off night when they arrived, all weary and discouraged, at the prison.

As for Nebuchadnezzar, he was much impressed; for of all the young men whom he had in training there were "none like Daniel, Hananiah, Mishael, and Azariah: therefore stood they before the king. And in all matters of wisdom and under-standing, that the king enquired of them, he found them ten times better than all the magicians and astrologers that were in all his realm."

Would you like to be "ten times better" than all the boys and girls in your school? Ten times wiser, ten times healthier, ten times nobler?

You can be. Just purpose in your heart to serve God always, whatever the cost.

STORY 2

The Forgotten Dream

THE MAGICIANS and astrologers who thronged Nebuchadnezzar's court and advised the king how to rule his empire were not at all pleased, I am sure, at the arrival of Daniel and his friends.

I can hear them saying to each other, under their breath, "Who are these young upstarts? Just out of school and think they know everything! Foreigners, too!"

But it was not long before they changed their minds about them.

One morning when the king took his seat upon his golden throne his servants noticed that his face wore a troubled look. Rumor spread that he had had a bad night and was in a very ugly mood.

That *something* had upset him was clear enough, but what it was no one knew, nor did anyone dare to ask. The servants guessed it was going to be a trying day for everybody, and they guessed right.

THE FORGOTTEN DREAM

Suddenly the king roused himself from his deep thought and snapped out a command.

"Summon my counselors!" he commanded. "Bring them all—the magicians, and the astrologers, and the sorcerers, and the Chaldeans."

Instantly the servants went into action. The king's command was carried by runners to all the wise men of Babylon.

Soon dozens of these important people, clad in their colorful robes of office, were hurrying to the palace, wondering what the king could want of them at such an hour. Was there bad news from the army in the field? Had revolution broken out somewhere? Or had the king merely thought of some new building he wanted to erect in the city?

One by one the counselors filed into the throne room and stood before the king. At once they noticed his troubled look and prepared for the worst.

When all had arrived the king began to speak—and then was everybody surprised!

He had not called them to consider any bad news from any part of his kingdom, nor did he want to talk about raising money for some great building scheme. He just wanted to tell them about a dream he had had!

At this everybody gave a sigh of relief. If it was only a dream that was troubling the king, they could soon put his mind at ease.

"O king, live for ever," said the chief of the Chaldeans, bowing low. "Tell thy servants the dream, and we will shew the interpretation."

6-2

PAINTING BY RUSSELL HARLAN   © 1955, BY REVIEW AND HERALD

In the dream that God sent him, Nebuchadnezzar saw a great image with a head of gold. Its
breast was of silver, its thighs of brass, its legs
of iron, and its toes part iron and part clay.

They were experts at spinning yarns about people's dreams and if only they could learn the king's dream, they could easily give some explanation of it. Unfortunately, the king couldn't remember his dream. Maybe you have had a similar experience. You have had a most vivid dream while you slept, but in the morning you couldn't remember anything about it. That is what happened to Nebuchadnezzar, and he was worried about it.

"No," he said to the wise men, "you tell *me* the dream. That's why I called you here."

Now the Chaldeans, the magicians, the astrologers, and the sorcerers looked at each other in alarm. Nobody had ever asked them to do such a thing. How could they know what a man dreamed about the night before? And they didn't dare guess, for they might guess wrong.

"I'll pay you well if you tell me," said the king. "I will see that you have gifts and rewards and great honor. But if you

don't, believe me, you shall be torn limb from limb and your houses shall be laid in ruins."

Again the Chaldeans pleaded that the king reveal his dream, and again the king told them what he would do if they didn't answer him, and soon.

"There is not a man upon the earth that can shew the king's matter," replied the Chaldeans. "There is no king, lord, nor ruler, that asked such things at any magician, or astrologer, or Chaldean. And it is a rare thing that the king requireth, and there is none other that can shew it before the king, except the gods, whose dwelling is not with flesh."

At this Nebuchadnezzar became furious. He had hoped that these men who claimed to know so much would easily recall a dream. Now it dawned upon him what cheap tricksters they were. They had been deceiving him all along. He was through with them. He wouldn't have them about his court any longer.

Hot with anger, he gave orders that all the wise men of Babylon should be killed.

STORY 3

Wonderful Prayer Meeting

F OR SOME reason or other Daniel and his three friends were not present with the other wise men when Nebuchadnezzar gave orders that they should be killed. But the king's command soon caught up with them.

There was a loud knock on their door. On opening it they saw Arioch, "the chief of the executioners," with a strong bodyguard of soldiers.

"What's the matter?" asked Daniel innocently, not knowing anything of what had happened that morning at court. "Why is the decree so hasty from the king?"

Arioch then told what had taken place. He was sorry, but orders were orders. Daniel and his friends would have to go with him.

Respectfully Daniel asked if he might see the king first and beg for a little time.

Arioch agreed. Why, it's hard to tell. But there was something so gentle, so gracious, and so modest about this young man that everybody loved him—even the chief executioner.

So Daniel went to see the king, promising him that if only he could have a little time he would tell him all he wanted to know.

Angry though he had been with the Chaldeans, the astrologers, the magicians, and the sorcerers, the king's heart softened at sight of this noble youth. He did not want Daniel to be killed, and so agreed to give him the time he asked.

Much depended on what Daniel did with the next few hours. Not only was his own life at stake, but the lives of his three friends and of all the wise men of Babylon.

What did he do? He ran to his house and told Hananiah, Mishael, and Azariah what the king had said. Then he suggested that they all fall on their knees and ask the great God of heaven, who knows everything, just what it was the king dreamed, and what was its meaning.

What a prayer meeting that was! How those four dear boys pleaded with God to help them, and soon, before the king's deadline should pass! I can almost hear them crying out, "Dear God, please, dear God, tell us the king's dream! Tell us what it means. Do not fail us! Help us, and help us now."

"Then was the secret revealed unto Daniel in a night vision."

That very night, right after that wonderful prayer meeting, Daniel saw the very same thing that Nebuchadnezzar had seen in his dream the night before. And as the marvelous picture passed before his eyes its meaning suddenly became plain to him. At once he understood why Nebuchadnezzar had been so troubled. God had been trying to tell him something of great importance about the future of his kingdom!

In the morning Daniel could hardly wait to tell the king what God had shown him. But first he told his friends, and together they thanked God for His goodness in answering their prayers so wonderfully and so soon.

"Blessed be the name of God for ever and ever," said Daniel.

"For wisdom and might are his: and he changeth the times and the seasons: he removeth kings, and setteth up kings: he giveth wisdom unto the wise, and knowledge to them that know understanding: he revealeth the deep and secret things: he knoweth what is in the darkness, and the light dwelleth with him. I thank thee, and praise thee, O thou God of my fathers, who hast given me wisdom and might, and hast made known unto me now what we desired of thee: for thou hast now made known unto us the king's matter."

Now Daniel hurried to Arioch, the chief executioner, with the good news. "Destroy not the wise men of Babylon," he urged: "bring me in before the king, and I will shew unto the king the interpretation."

The look on Daniel's face, and the gleam in his eye, told Arioch that the young man meant what he said.

"I'll take you," he said. "And hurry; there's not much time."

So Arioch "brought in Daniel before the king in haste."

Trying to take a little glory to himself, the chief executioner said, "I have found a man of the captives of Judah, that will make known unto the king the interpretation."

But the king took no notice of Arioch. His eyes were fixed on the splendid youth who stood before him, upon whose face glowed a light never seen in Babylon before.

Surely this was the same young man who but yesterday had come to him and asked for time! Here he was back again already! What had he to say now?

Daniel's great moment had come.

23

STORY 4

Image That Vanished

LOOKING earnestly at Daniel, King Nebuchadnezzar asked him, "Can you tell me my dream and what it means?"

"No," said Daniel, humbly. "There is no man wise enough to do such a thing; but there is a God in heaven who reveals secrets and He has made known to Your Majesty what will happen in the latter days."

"But my dream!" said the king. "What did I dream?"

"In your·dream," said Daniel, "you were thinking about things to come to pass hereafter."

"That's right; I was!" said the king. "I was wondering what will happen to my kingdom after I am dead."

Leaning forward, he gazed intently at the remarkable young man before him. Somehow he felt sure he was about to discover what he had been seeking so long.

Calmly, respectfully, Daniel went on.

"You saw a great image," he said. "This great image,

whose brightness was excellent, stood before you, and the form thereof was terrible."

The king almost leaped from his throne. This was it—the very thing he had been trying so hard to recall! A huge metallic man. It had stood by his bed and glared down at him. He would never forget it again as long as he lived.

"This image's head," continued Daniel, "was of fine gold, his breast and his arms of silver, his belly and thighs of brass, his legs of iron, his feet part of iron and part of clay."

"Exactly!" cried the king. "That is just what I saw."

"Yes," said Daniel, "and you watched it till a stone, cut out without hands, smote the image upon its feet that were of iron and clay, and broke them to pieces.

"Then was the iron, the clay, the brass, the silver, and the gold, broken to pieces together, and became like the chaff of the summer threshingfloors; and the wind carried them away, that no place was found for them."

"That's right!" said the king. "The whole thing suddenly disappeared, as though the wind had blown it away."

"Yes; and the stone took its place," said Daniel. "Indeed it became a great mountain, and filled the whole earth."

"It did! It did!" cried the king, overcome with amazement.

This was too marvelous! How could this youth know so much? Everything he had said was right. Every little detail was correct. He had not made a single mistake. Surely the God whom he served must be a wonderful God if He could recall a man's dream like this.

But what did it all mean? How did it reveal the future? What had it to do with the latter days?

Nebuchadnezzar could hardly wait to learn the meaning of this strange and terrible thing he had seen in the night.

Why was the image made of several different metals? Why did it have a head of gold but feet of iron and clay? Why was it broken to pieces? Why did it vanish so suddenly, blown away by the wind? What was the magic stone that smashed gold, silver, brass, and iron to pieces as though they were nothing but pottery—then suddenly grew and grew and grew into a great mountain that filled the whole earth?

What mighty mysteries were here! Could the young man solve them?

Breathlessly the king waited for Daniel to speak again.

STORY 5

Vision of the Future

IN THE same calm, serious voice Daniel went on to tell Nebuchadnezzar the meaning of the strange metallic image he had seen in his dream.

"You are this head of gold," said the young man, and a smile of satisfaction flickered on the king's face. He was flattered that the glory of his empire should be mentioned first.

But Babylon, strong and proud though it was at the moment, would not last forever.

Said Daniel, "After you shall arise another kingdom, not so great as yours." This was the meaning of the "breast and arms of silver."

Then a third world empire would arise, pictured by the "belly and thighs of brass." This in turn would be overthrown by a fourth kingdom, strong as iron, like the two legs of the image.

As the feet and toes were made "part of iron and part of clay" so the fourth kingdom would be divided into several

27

kingdoms, some weak, some strong, and they would remain divided until the God of heaven, the King of kings, should come to set up His everlasting kingdom.

"Whereas you saw the feet and toes," said Daniel, "part of potters' clay and part of iron, the kingdom shall be divided. They shall not cleave one to another, even as iron is not mixed with clay.

"And in the days of these kings shall the God of heaven set up a kingdom, which shall never be destroyed: and the kingdom shall not be left to other people, but it shall break in pieces and consume all these kingdoms, and it shall stand for ever."

As Daniel talked on, Nebuchadnezzar forgot that he was sitting in the throne room of Babylon. It seemed to him that he was standing at an open window, looking down the ages upon the great events of history to be.

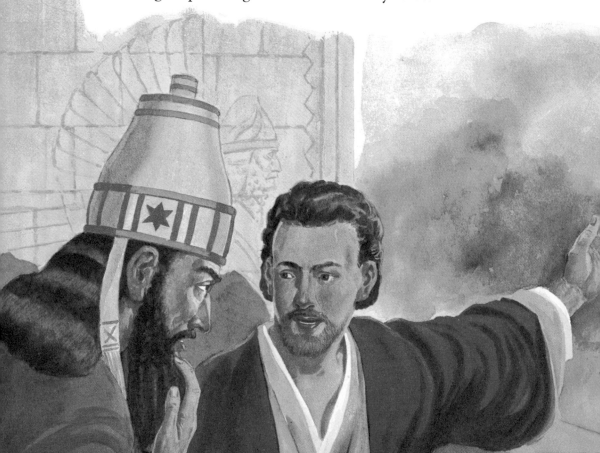

VISION OF THE FUTURE

And he was. In fact, both king and prophet, lord and slave, were looking through the window of the future. Before them stretched the wondrous panorama of all the years to come. Close by them they saw the golden temples of Babylon. Beyond, stretching far into the distance, were the silver minarets of Medo-Persia, the brazen towers of Grecia, and the iron domes of Rome.

On, on down the ages they peered, till they saw the mighty Roman Empire divided into the nations of modern Europe. They saw these nations fighting each other in great and terrible wars, as strong leaders tried in vain to unite them into one great whole again.

Then, "in the days of these kings"—that is, in our day—they saw something tremendous happen. Suddenly their eyes were drawn from earth to heaven, and there in the sky they beheld a great fiery glow as the King of kings descended in mighty power to bring all earthly empires to an end.

Wonderful vision! How their hearts must have thrilled at the sight! When it was over, the mighty king of Babylon "fell upon his face" before his Hebrew slave whom God had so wonderfully used to reveal the future to him. "Of a truth," he cried, "your God is a God of gods, and a Lord of kings, and a revealer of secrets, seeing that thou couldest reveal this secret."

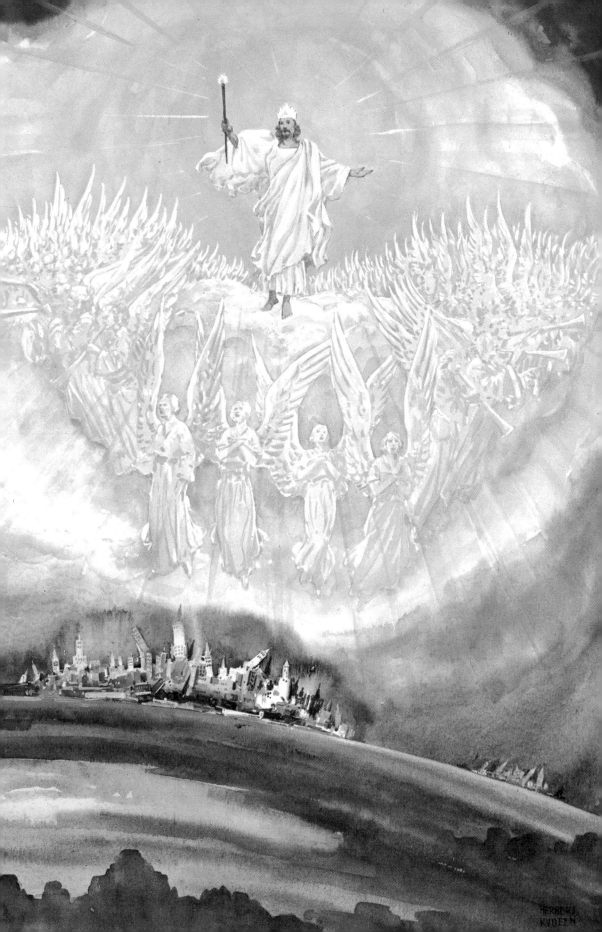

"Then the king made Daniel a great man, and gave him many great gifts, and made him ruler over the whole province of Babylon, and chief of the governors over all the wise men of Babylon."

Thus, though Jerusalem was in ruins, and all the children of Israel were in captivity, God was still at work in the earth. The king of Judah may have refused to listen to Him, but in the king of Babylon He found a ready listener.

As His messenger He used one of the captive Israelites, a lad who had purposed in his heart to serve Him at all costs. Now, having proved Daniel's loyalty, God caused him to be made "ruler over the whole province of Babylon" and "chief of the governors." Here, next to King Nebuchadnezzar in authority, he could watch over the interests of God's people until the time to free them should come.

So, though for a while it must have seemed to the children of Israel that all was lost and that God had forsaken them forever, it wasn't really so. Though they had failed Him miserably He was still, in His own wonderful way, working His purpose out.

Nebuchadnezzar's dream about the image was meant not only for this heathen king, but for Daniel and all his people. It told them in the strongest possible way that in the long struggle with evil God is bound to win. Comforting indeed was its message that when the empires of the world have run their course God's reign will have just begun.

STORY 6

The Golden Idol

≋≋≋≋≋≋≋≋≋≋≋≋≋≋≋≋

THAT dream of the metallic image made a great impression on Nebuchadnezzar. For though at first he couldn't remember it, after Daniel had brought it back to his mind and explained its meaning he couldn't think of anything else.

But there was one thing about it he didn't like. That was the suggestion that his great empire would someday give place to another. He wondered whether that had to be. Perhaps if he made Babylon strong enough he could stop anything like that from happening.

Then he had a bright idea. He would make an image like the one he had seen in his dream, but of *one* metal, not several, to show that his kingdom would last forever. Not just the head would be of gold but the entire body—arms, legs, feet, toes, everything.

So he gave orders for the work to be carried out. And what a gigantic image it was! When completed it stood about

100 feet tall, including its pedestal, while the width at the shoulders was more than ten feet. Imagine it! And all of gold!

Crowds must have gathered to watch as the great gleaming idol was carried out of the city and set up in the midst of the plain of Dura. Soldiers no doubt went along to guard it and see that thieves didn't break off its golden toes at night.

Everybody wondered what the king planned to do with so huge an image in such a place, but they did not have long to wait to find out. Soon word spread everywhere that Nebuchadnezzar had sent messengers throughout the whole Babylonian empire commanding the princes, the governors, and the captains, the judges, the treasurers, and the counselors, the sheriffs, and all the rulers of the provinces, to come to the dedication of the image.

THE GOLDEN IDOL

One and all they came; and a great sight it must have been as all these important officials, each with his train of servants, began to arrive in the capital.

When the day of dedication arrived tens of thousands gathered on the plain of Dura, men and women, boys and girls. Some no doubt camped out all the previous night to get a place with a good view. Others started coming at early dawn, bringing their lunches with them.

Everyone was excited—especially the children—for wasn't the king himself coming to the show and the royal band providing the music?

More and more people arrived. The crowd became thicker and thicker, especially towards the center, where the great golden image towered above all.

Suddenly a hush fell over the mighty throng. A richly dressed herald began to speak.

Slowly, in a loud, clear voice, he cried, "To you it is commanded, O people, nations, and languages, that at what time ye hear the sound of the cornet, flute, harp, sackbut, psaltery, dulcimer, and all kinds of musick, ye fall down and worship the golden image that Nebuchadnezzar the king hath set up."

Then he added this warning: "Whoso falleth not down and worshippeth shall the same hour be cast into the midst of a burning fiery furnace."

Then the band began to play. Just what sort of tune came from those cornets, flutes, harps, sackbuts, psalteries, and other musical instruments we are not told, but as the sound rolled out over the plain, the people with one accord fell on their faces before the image.

Nebuchadnezzar, looking over the amazing scene from his royal throne, felt very pleased with himself. This was just what he had planned! Everybody bowing down to his image. No, no, his empire would never pass away. Not with such obedience as this—and a little touch of the fiery furnace to help things along!

His contentment did not last long, however, for far out in the kneeling crowd he noticed a disturbance. Some people were actually standing. Yes, *standing!*

"What's the matter?" he demanded of those about him.

"It's Shadrach, Meshach, and Abednego, Your Majesty," said his Chaldean counselors. "You know, those three young

THE GOLDEN IDOL

Hebrews whom you promoted not long ago. They refuse to bow down to your golden image."

"What!" cried Nebuchadnezzar in a rage. "Bring them here. I'll teach them to disobey me!"

Soldiers brought the three young men through the crowd while everybody looked up to see what was going on. Quickly the news spread. Voices buzzed. "Did you see *that!*" one said to another. "Three young men refused to bow to the golden idol! They've been arrested and taken before the king. Whatever will happen to them?"

By this time the people were far more interested in the three young Hebrews than ever they had been in the image. The dedication was completely spoiled.

STORY 7

Thrown to the Flames

ONLY a few people close to the royal enclosure could see and hear what happened next, but everybody tried to. While the great golden image still towered above them the crowds surged forward to catch a glimpse of the three young men who had dared to defy the king. Many a little boy, I am sure, climbed on his daddy's shoulders to get a better view of what was going on.

"Is it true?" asked Nebuchadnezzar of Shadrach, Meshach, and Abednego. "Do not ye serve my gods, nor worship the golden image which I have set up?"

Then he offered them one more chance, for he had liked these young men from the first time he had seen them. The band would play again. If they would now fall down before the image all would be well. If not, they would be cast at once into "a burning fiery furnace." "And what God," asked the king, "shall deliver you out of my hands?"

It was an awful moment for the three young men. Nobody

likes to be burned alive. They could see smoke rising from the furnace which the king had brought along to deal with people like them, and they knew very well that he would do exactly as he had said if they disobeyed him again. Yet they did not flinch.

They could have said to themselves, "Well, just bowing down once won't matter very much. We wouldn't really be worshiping the image. We would just do it to please the king who has been so good to us." But they did no such thing. They remembered the commandment of God, "Thou shalt not make unto thee any graven image . . . : thou shalt not bow down thyself to them, nor serve them." And they decided that they must obey God rather than man.

"O Nebuchadnezzar," they said respectfully, "our God whom we serve is able to deliver us from the burning fiery furnace, and he will deliver us out of thine hand, O king. But if not, be it known unto thee, O king, that we will not serve thy gods, nor worship the golden image which thou hast set up."

At this the king became very furious and could hardly contain his rage.

"Heat the furnace!" he roared. "Make it seven times hotter than it ever was heated before!"

THROWN TO THE FLAMES

Servants ran to do his bidding. Some started to throw more fuel on the fire. Others worked the bellows to fan the flames to white heat. Meanwhile the strongest men in the king's army were called to bind the three young men with ropes.

Hotter and hotter grew the fire, until the king and the whole royal party could feel the heat of it. Now the problem arose as to how to get the young men into it. It was too hot. Nobody could get near it. Even the mighty men who had bound Shadrach, Meshach, and Abednego drew back, wondering what to do next.

"Throw them in!" yelled the king in his wild anger.

The soldiers obeyed. Picking up the three young men, they moved forward, threw them into the furnace, then fell to the ground and died from the terrible heat.

Nebuchadnezzar did not care. His foolish jealousy was now satisfied. Nobody would dare disobey him again. As for the three young Hebrews and their God he was glad to be rid of them.

Suddenly a cry was raised.

"Look! There's somebody in the fire!"

"What!" cried the king. "Impossible!"

But there was.

Wide-eyed with amazement he gazed through the open doors of the blazing furnace.

Yes, there *was* somebody inside it. Two people in fact. No, three, four!

Others were looking now; everybody who could get close enough to peer in.

41

hadrach, Meshach, and Abednego had been
rown into the fiery furnace for refusing to
ow down to the great image, but the king
embled to see the Son of God among them.

"Did we not cast three men bound into the midst of the fire?" cried the king.

"True, O king," said those about him.

"Lo, I see four men loose, walking in the midst of the fire, and they have no hurt; and the form of the fourth is like the Son of God."

Forgetting his royal dignity, forgetting the tens of thousands of eyes that were upon him, Nebuchadnezzar left his throne and hurried as near as he dared to the door of the furnace.

"Shadrach, Meshach, and Abednego!" he cried. "Ye servants of the most high God, come forth, and come hither."

They came.

They were not burned in any way, nor were their clothes

even scorched. All that the fire had consumed were the ropes that had bound them.

Everybody crowded round to see the astounding sight. "And the princes, governors, and captains, and the king's counsellors, being gathered together, saw these men, upon whose bodies the fire had no power, nor was an hair of their head singed, neither were their coats changed, nor the smell of fire had passed on them."

How much the vast crowd saw of all this we do not know. But we can be sure that the amazing story was told and retold ten thousand times that day.

As for Nebuchadnezzar, he was quite overcome by the experience. He never said another word about his great golden idol. Instead, he declared to all about him, "Blessed be the God of Shadrach, Meshach, and Abednego, who hath sent his angel, and delivered his servants that trusted in him, and have changed the king's word, and yielded their bodies, that they might not serve or worship any god, except their own God.

"Therefore I make a decree, That every people, nation, and language, which speak anything amiss against the God of Shadrach, Meshach, and Abednego, shall be cut in pieces, and their houses shall be made a dunghill: because there is no other God that can deliver after this sort."

It was indeed a wonderful deliverance, and God used it to cheer the hearts of His people in the days of their captivity. It must have been a comfort to them to know that He was willing to walk in the fire with those three dear faithful lads!

Perhaps He will do the same for you someday.

STORY 8

The King Goes Mad

YEARS rolled by. Nebuchadnezzar kept on building up Babylon and extending his empire. He became stronger and stronger, richer and still more rich.

By now he had become quite sure that Daniel had been wrong in saying that his kingdom would pass away and that another would arise to take its place. That might have been possible at the beginning of his reign, but not now. Look at his army! Note the height of the walls of his fortress capital! See all the people he had conquered! No enemy could take all this from him now!

Then it was that he had another dream. This one he did not forget, but he couldn't understand it.

Strangely enough, it was about a tree. At first the tree was small, but it grew and grew until its branches reached far up into the sky. It bore much fruit, and many animals took shelter in its shade.

Then he saw an angel come down from heaven crying,

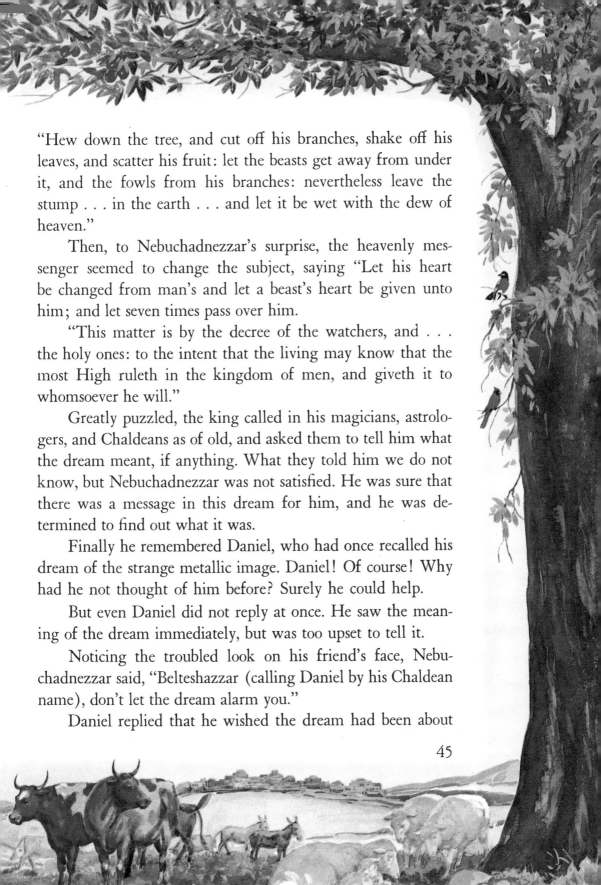

"Hew down the tree, and cut off his branches, shake off his leaves, and scatter his fruit: let the beasts get away from under it, and the fowls from his branches: nevertheless leave the stump . . . in the earth . . . and let it be wet with the dew of heaven."

Then, to Nebuchadnezzar's surprise, the heavenly messenger seemed to change the subject, saying "Let his heart be changed from man's and let a beast's heart be given unto him; and let seven times pass over him.

"This matter is by the decree of the watchers, and . . . the holy ones: to the intent that the living may know that the most High ruleth in the kingdom of men, and giveth it to whomsoever he will."

Greatly puzzled, the king called in his magicians, astrologers, and Chaldeans as of old, and asked them to tell him what the dream meant, if anything. What they told him we do not know, but Nebuchadnezzar was not satisfied. He was sure that there was a message in this dream for him, and he was determined to find out what it was.

Finally he remembered Daniel, who had once recalled his dream of the strange metallic image. Daniel! Of course! Why had he not thought of him before? Surely he could help.

But even Daniel did not reply at once. He saw the meaning of the dream immediately, but was too upset to tell it.

Noticing the troubled look on his friend's face, Nebuchadnezzar said, "Belteshazzar (calling Daniel by his Chaldean name), don't let the dream alarm you."

Daniel replied that he wished the dream had been about

45

the king's enemies, rather than about the king himself. Then he told Nebuchadnezzar what the dream meant.

"The tree is yourself," he said. "You have grown and become strong and your kingdom reaches to the ends of the earth. But by the decree of the most High you shall be driven from your palace and made to live among the beasts of the field. You will eat grass as they do, and your body will be wet with the dew. For seven years this will continue, until you admit that the most High rules in the kingdom of men and gives it to whomever He will."

This was a terrible thing to say to a king in those days—especially one with a temper like Nebuchadnezzar's, but Daniel was never afraid of doing his duty. Then, seeing the king was deeply moved, he added with great tenderness, "Wherefore, O king, accept my counsel: Break off your sins by right-

eousness, and your iniquities by showing mercy to the poor."

The king listened thoughtfully. Perhaps for a moment he thought he would do as Daniel had said. But as the days and weeks went by he drifted back into his old ways. He was still too proud to make God first in his life.

"At the end of twelve months he walked in the palace of the kingdom of Babylon" saying to himself, "Is not this great Babylon, that I have built for the house of the kingdom by the might of my power, and for the honour of my majesty?"

Then, suddenly, "while the word was in the king's mouth, there fell a voice from heaven, saying, O king Nebuchadnezzar; to thee it is spoken; The kingdom is departed from thee. . . .

"The same hour was the thing fulfilled upon Nebuchadnezzar: and he was driven from men, and did eat grass as oxen, and his body was wet with the dew of heaven, till his

47

hairs were grown like eagles' feathers, and his nails like birds' claws."

In other words, he became mad and lived like an animal out in the fields.

At the end of seven years he became sane again. Here is the amazing story in his own words: "At the end of the days I Nebuchadnezzar lifted up mine eyes unto heaven, and mine understanding returned unto me, and I blessed the most High, and I praised and honoured him that liveth for ever, whose dominion is an everlasting dominion, and his kingdom is from generation to generation: and all the inhabitants of the earth are reputed as nothing: and he doeth according to his will in the army of heaven, and among the inhabitants of the earth: and none can stay his hand, or say unto him, What doest thou?

"At the same time my reason returned unto me; and . . . I was established in my kingdom, and excellent majesty was added unto me.

"Now I Nebuchadnezzar praise and extol and honour the King of heaven, all whose works are truth, and his ways judgment: and those that walk in pride he is able to abase."

So Nebuchadnezzar, one of the most famous kings of ancient times, found his way to God. He learned how foolish it is to be proud, to take glory to oneself. Humbly he admitted that he—though king of Babylon—was nobody at all in the presence of the Lord of heaven. Gladly he agreed that God is in charge of the affairs of this world and that "the heavens do rule." Maybe some of us need to learn the same lesson today.

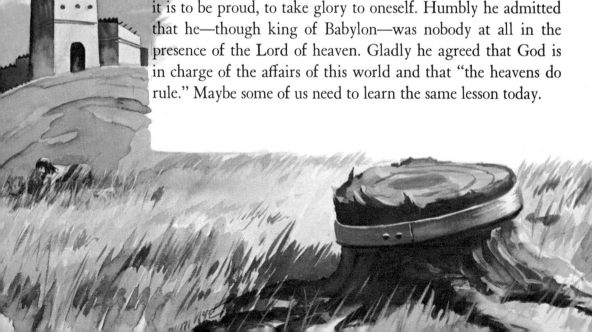

STORY 9

Writing on the Wall

HOW LONG Nebuchadnezzar lived after he made his decree praising the King of heaven we are not told. Some say one year, some say more. But we do know that when he died the glory of Babylon died with him.

His son, Evil-Merodach, was a weak king, as were those who followed him. They lived for pleasure, forgetting that there were powerful enemies waiting for the first signs of the empire's decay.

Not long after Belshazzar came to the throne he called all the leading men of his kingdom to a great feast in the royal palace. At least a thousand came, and the best food and wine in Babylon were brought to the tables.

A heavy drinker himself, Belshazzar set the worst possible example before his guests. Soon many of them were drunk, behaving shamelessly as people do when they have taken too much wine.

As the night wore on, the scene in the banqueting hall

became more and more wild and noisy. Men and women shouted the praises of the gods of Babylon and drank again and again in their honor. There were music, singing, and dancing as the feast moved to its climax.

By and by the king, very drunk himself, ordered his servants to bring the gold and silver vessels that Nebuchadnezzar had taken out of the Temple at Jerusalem nearly seventy years before. With laughter and joking they were passed to the people at the king's table. Wine was poured into them. The king and his guests drank it, jeering at the God to whom these vessels once were dedicated.

Suddenly a cry of fear rang through the hall. All eyes turned toward Belshazzar. He had risen to his feet and was pointing toward something on the palace wall.

"L-l-look!" he cried. "Over there! By the candlestick! See, a hand is writing on the wall!"

Dead silence fell. The banquet was forgotten as everyone looked in the direction the king was pointing.

"What is it?" whispered some, pale with fright.

"A hand!" cried others. "See! There it is! Over there! Over there!"

Soon all saw the terrifying sight. Screams of horror arose.

Slowly the mystic fingers moved across the wall, leaving a message written in letters of fire that blazed in the semi-darkness of the banqueting hall.

Shaking from head to foot, his knees knocking together, Belshazzar shouted for his astrologers, Chaldeans, and sooth-sayers to come forward and read the writing.

They came. But even though the king promised them great riches and honor, they could not tell what the writing meant.

Everybody was worried now. That this was some evil portent they were sure. But of what? Some guessed one thing and some another.

Swiftly the story swept through the palace, as terrified servants passed it from one to another.

"It was awful!" they cried. "We saw it ourselves! . . . The fingers of a man's hand writing on the wall!"

"Nonsense!"

"Go and see for yourself! The writing is still there! The king will make you the third ruler in the land if you can read it to him."

A maid burst into the bedchamber of the queen mother, daughter of Nebuchadnezzar. Breathlessly she told what had happened and how the king was almost out of his mind with fright and worry.

The queen mother decided to go and see for herself. The writing was still there. She took one look, then turned to Belshazzar and bade him not to worry. "Call Daniel," she said. "He will tell you what it means."

Ever since she was a little girl she had known and loved Daniel. It could be that he had told her about her father's dreams and their meaning.

"The spirit of the holy gods is in him," she said. "Nebuchadnezzar made him master of the magicians. He can interpret dreams and dissolve doubts. Call him."

So, even though it must have been far past midnight, the king sent for Daniel.

Soon the prophet arrived, now an old, bearded man more than eighty years of age.

Said Belshazzar: "If you can read this writing, I will clothe you in scarlet, put a chain of gold around your neck, and make you the third ruler in the kingdom."

"Keep your gifts," said Daniel. "Yet I will read the writing for you."

And this he did. But first he told the king what God thought of all his wicked ways.

"O thou king," he said, "the most high God gave Nebu-

chadnezzar thy father a kingdom, and majesty, and glory, and honour. . . . But when his heart was lifted up, and his mind hardened in pride, he was deposed from his kingly throne, and they took his glory from him:

"And he was driven from the sons of men; and . . . they fed him with grass like oxen, and his body was wet with the dew of heaven; till he knew that the most high God ruled in the kingdom of men. . . .

"And thou his son, O Belshazzar, hast not humbled thine heart, though thou knewest all this; but hast lifted up thyself against the Lord of heaven; and they have brought the vessels of his house before thee, and thou, and thy lords . . . have drunk wine in them; and thou hast praised the gods of silver, and gold, of brass, iron, wood, and stone, which see not, nor hear, nor know: and the God in whose hand thy breath is, and whose are all thy ways, hast thou not glorified:

"Then was the part of the hand sent from him; and this writing was written."

So it was the God of heaven who had sent this message! The hand of an angel had written on the wall!

White with fear, still trembling from head to foot, the king waited to hear what God had said.

"This is the writing that was written," said Daniel, "MENE, MENE, TEKEL, UPHARSIN."

Then he told the meaning. It ran like this:

"God hath numbered thy kingdom, and finished it."

"Thou art weighed in the balances, and art found wanting."

53

"Thy kingdom is divided, and given to the Medes and Persians."

There was a pause. All eyes turned from Daniel to Belshazzar. What would he do now?

"Bring the scarlet robe," the king commanded, "and the chain of gold. This man shall be the third ruler in the kingdom."

Even as he spoke, however, loud shouts and the clash of swords came through the open windows of the banqueting hall.

"To arms! To arms!" cried the king. "The enemy is upon us!"

It was too late. Drunken guards had left the city gates open. Now the Medo-Persian soldiers were swarming everywhere, with no one able to resist them.

That night Babylon fell, Belshazzar was killed, "and Darius the Median took the kingdom."

STORY 10

Night With the Lions

WHEN the Medo-Persians took possession of Babylon they found Daniel in his house, but did not kill him. Instead, learning that he had just been made the third ruler of the kingdom, they took him before Darius.

It could well be that the new king had already heard of Daniel during the many years that this famous Hebrew slave was Nebuchadnezzar's prime minister. Certain it is that as they talked together the old man made a deep impression upon Darius. So much so that when the king made up his new government and "set over the kingdom an hundred and twenty princes" he appointed Daniel the first of three presidents in charge of them.

Unfortunately the other two presidents and the hundred and twenty princes did not like this plan. They thought it most unfair that anyone who had held an important position in Babylon should be put ahead of good, loyal Medo-Persians.

These jealous men did their best to get rid of Daniel. They spread wicked rumors about him, charging him with being a traitor and accusing him of one wrong thing after another. But they couldn't prove any of their charges.

Every time they tried to build up a case against him it collapsed. "Forasmuch as he was faithful, neither was there any error or fault found in him." Daniel was so honest, so true, so loyal, that these men finally said to each other, "We shall find nothing against him unless it has to do with his religion."

Knowing that Daniel never failed to say his prayers three times a day—morning, noon, and night—they plotted together to persuade King Darius to issue a decree that no one should ask a petition "of any God or man" save himself, for the next thirty days, the penalty being death in the den of lions.

Darius, much flattered by the suggestion, signed the decree.

Then someone came and told Daniel. He saw through the wicked scheme at once. But did he alter his lifelong plan of daily worship? Did he decide to give up saying his prayers, or to whisper them secretly, out of sight? No, not he! He had witnessed for God all his life in this heathen city, and he was not going to give up now. If it meant dying in the den of lions, all right, let it be so. He would be faithful unto death.

So "when Daniel knew that the writing was signed, he went into his house; and his windows being open in his chamber toward Jerusalem, he kneeled upon his knees three times a day, and prayed, and gave thanks before God, as he did aforetime."

People were used to seeing Daniel praying at that window,

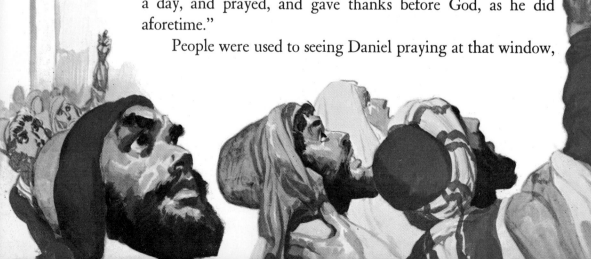

but now they crowded the
street before his house to witness
his quiet defiance of the new law.

"Look at him!" they cried. "Doesn't
he know about the king's decree?"

"He'll know when he finds himself in the den
of lions," said others.

Meanwhile the jealous princes hurried to Darius with the
story. Now, too late, the king realized what they had led him
to do. He was very angry, but having made the decree, there
was nothing he could do but order that Daniel be thrown to
the lions.

So Daniel was arrested and led through the streets to
the den.

What a procession that must have been! The aged
prophet out in front, followed by the princes and many soldiers.
Thousands of men and women, boys and girls, looked on,
many of them sad that this dear old man was going to be killed.
But Daniel strode on unmoved, his trust in God unshaken.

The door of the den was opened. Daniel walked in. But
the lions did not touch him. Instead they slunk away, as though
afraid of him. All that night, while Daniel prayed, they paced
to and fro, growling now and then, but never trying to attack
him.

Early in the morning Daniel heard a familiar voice

57

calling to him from outside the den. It was the king!

"Daniel, Daniel," cried Darius, "servant of the living God, is thy God, whom thou servest continually, able to deliver thee from the lions?"

Oh, yes, indeed. Well able.

Said Daniel, "My God hath sent his angel, and hath shut the lions' mouths, that they have not hurt me."

"Then was the king exceeding glad for him, and commanded that they should take Daniel up out of the den. . . . And no manner of hurt was found upon him, because he believed in his God."

Some may say that the lions did not touch Daniel because they weren't hungry. Oh, but they were! When those who had found fault with Daniel were put in his place there was a terrible scene. The lions pounced on them at once, breaking all their bones in pieces before they reached the bottom of the den.

King Darius was so impressed by what happened that night that he sent a special message to everybody in his kingdom, saying, "I make a decree, That in every dominion of my kingdom men tremble and fear before the God of Daniel: for he is the living God, and stedfast for ever. . . .

"He delivereth and rescueth, and he worketh signs and wonders in heaven and in earth, who hath delivered Daniel from the power of the lions."

This wonderful message comes down across the centuries to you and me. For the God who lived in Daniel's day is just the same today. "Stedfast for ever," He still delivers and rescues those who trust in Him.

59

← PAINTING BY KREIGH COLLINS   © 1955, BY REVIEW AND HERALD

Because Daniel continued to pray to the true God, whom he had worshiped all his life, he was thrown into a den of lions, but an angel protected him by shutting the lions' mouths.

STORY 11

Animals From the Sea

WHEN I was a very little boy I used to have a strange dream every now and then. All sorts of wild animals would come walking up the big staircase in my home and file past my bedroom door. I particularly remember the giraffes, because their heads knocked against the ceiling, high though it was.

Well, Daniel once had a dream like that, only his animals didn't come upstairs; they walked out of the sea.

One night, not long before he was called to read the writing on the wall at Belshazzar's feast, he had a vision of the seaside. Maybe it was a rocky strip of coast such as he remembered seeing in Palestine, or a sandy beach like that beside the Persian Gulf, which he must have passed many times in his travels on the king's business.

A fierce wind was blowing, and great waves were thundering on the shore.

Suddenly, as he stood there gazing at the wild surf,

ANIMALS FROM THE SEA

he saw a strange-looking animal coming out of the water. It wasn't a whale, or a shark, or a porpoise, such as might have been washed in by a storm. No, it was a lion. But not an ordinary lion, for it had eagle's wings.

As the lion drew nearer, a fierce gust of wind seemed to tear off its wings, whereupon the queer animal rose on its hind legs and behaved more like a man than a lion.

At this point Daniel became aware that a second beast was coming out of the sea. This was a bear, not walking as bears usually do, but sort of humped up on one side; and it had three ribs in its mouth, as though it were hungry.

Then came a leopard, with four heads and four wings of a fowl.

Hardly had this strange creature passed by when there was a fearful commotion out in the surf. Now Daniel saw a fourth beast so "dreadful and terrible" that he couldn't think of a name for it. It had ten horns and great iron teeth. It was "strong exceedingly" and stamped its feet madly on the shore.

As Daniel gazed in astonishment he saw another horn appear and gradually grow bigger. It had eyes and a mouth, and it pulled up three of the other horns by the roots.

Looking upward at this moment the old prophet seemed to see right into heaven. In his vision he saw God, "the Ancient of days," seated upon a glorious throne. "A fiery stream issued and came forth from before him: thousand thousands ministered unto him, and ten thousand times ten thousand stood before him: the judgment was set, and the books were opened."

The judgment! And who was being judged? Daniel listened intently. The angels were talking about the four strange beasts and particularly about the last one, which had been so evil looking.

In the books were recorded all the cruel, unkind things it had done, and Daniel was amazed at the number of them. Finally he heard the verdict: Guilty! And the penalty, Death! He said: "I beheld even till the beast was slain, and his body destroyed, and given to the burning flame."

Then a lovely thing happened. So different. So beautiful. "One like the Son of man came with the clouds of heaven, and came to the Ancient of days, and they brought him near before him."

Now there was great rejoicing in heaven as there was given to this glorious Being "dominion, and glory, and a kingdom, that all people, nations, and languages, should serve him."

It was a happy ending to what had begun as a strange and terrifying dream.

ANIMALS FROM THE SEA

But what was the meaning of all these wonderful things?

That is what Daniel wanted to know. The Bible says that he was greatly troubled about them.

Then an angel came and explained everything. What Daniel had seen, he said, was really a vision of things to come. God had allowed him to look into the future.

The four strange beasts that rose out of the sea stood for four great empires that would follow one another in years to come. The lion was Babylon, whose wings were already plucked. The bear represented Medo-Persia, whose armies were already approaching Babylon. After that would come Greece, the leopard beast, followed in turn by Rome and the horns, or powers, that would grow out of it.

These world empires, especially the fourth, would do many terrible things; but God in heaven would be watching them all the time, while angels would record in the books of heaven all that they said or did.

Someday there would be a judgment. Then all world powers that had done evil, or had hurt God's people in any way, would be found guilty, sentenced to death and destruction. In their place God would set up His own kingdom of love, righteousness, and peace, with "one like the Son of man" as its glorious and eternal King.

"And the kingdom and dominion, and the greatness of the kingdom under the whole heaven, shall be given to the people of the saints of the most High, whose kingdom is an everlasting kingdom, and all dominions shall serve and obey him."

Come to think of it, that was a very wonderful thing that happened that night in far-off Babylon. Jerusalem was still in ruins; the children of Israel were still in captivity; yet here was God saying to his faithful old servant, "Kings may come and kings may go; empires may rise and fall; but I have not forgotten My people nor My purpose. Someday all will come out right. Someday the Seed of the woman will bruise the serpent's head; someday all people on the earth will love and serve Me; someday Eden will be restored."

STORY 12

Gabriel's Glorious Secret

TIME and again through the long years of their captivity in Babylon the children of Israel must have thought about their homeland and wondered when they would see it again.

Some remembered Jeremiah's prophecy that they would return after seventy years. But it didn't seem possible that anything so wonderful could ever happen.

The first captives, taken by Nebuchadnezzar, grew older and older. Many died. The others counted the years. Forty. Fifty. Sixty. Sixty-five. Sixty-six. Sixty-seven. Sixty-eight. Would God remember? Would He set them free as He had promised?

One day Daniel was reading again the precious scroll containing the writings of Jeremiah. Once more he came to the passage: "After seventy years be accomplished at Babylon I will visit you, and perform my good word toward you, in causing you to return to this place.

66

"For I know the thoughts that I think toward you, saith the Lord, thoughts of peace, and not of evil, to give you an expected end.

"Then ye shall call upon me, and ye shall go and pray unto me, and I will hearken unto you.

"And ye shall seek me, and find me, when ye shall search for me with all your heart."

What beautiful words! What loving-kindness, what tender forgiveness there was in them! How thoughtful of God to give His people "an expected end"—something to hope for, even in their darkest days!

Suddenly Daniel was struck by the thought that the time for the fulfillment of the promise must be very near. Had he not been in Babylon himself almost seventy years? Perhaps, old as he was, he would see Jerusalem again!

What was it God had said His people must do? "Ye shall call upon me, and . . . pray unto me."

Daniel fell upon his knees and prayed one of the most beautiful prayers to be found in the Bible.

"O Lord, the great and dreadful God," he cried, "keeping the covenant and mercy to them that love him, and to them that

keep his commandments; we have sinned, . . . neither have we hearkened unto thy servants the prophets, which spake in thy name to our kings, our princes, and our fathers, and to all the people of the land. . . .

"O Lord, according to all thy righteousness, I beseech thee, let thine anger and thy fury be turned away from thy city Jerusalem, thy holy mountain. . . . Cause thy face to shine upon thy sanctuary that is desolate, for the Lord's sake. . . .

"O Lord, hear; O Lord, forgive; O Lord, hearken and do; defer not, for thine own sake, O my God: for thy city and thy people are called by thy name."

Just then, as he was praying, Daniel felt a touch upon his shoulder. Looking up, he saw an angel. It was Gabriel,

who had flown from heaven in the few brief moments since Daniel had begun to pray.

"You are greatly beloved," said Gabriel, "and I have come to tell you a secret."

Daniel was not to worry about Jerusalem. A commandment would be given to rebuild it. God would keep the promise He had made through Jeremiah. But just now He was planning the future, and how He would work out His grand design to bring evil to an end and make the earth like Eden again.

Daniel had been thinking about seventy years, but God was thinking of seven times seventy years—seventy weeks of years—that would reach far down the stream of time to the greatest thing He would ever do in His conflict with Satan.

"Seventy weeks," said Gabriel, "are determined upon thy people and upon thy holy city, to finish the transgression, and to make an end of sins, and to make reconciliation for iniquity, and to bring in everlasting righteousness, and to seal up the vision and prophecy, and to anoint the most Holy.

"Know therefore and understand, that from the going forth of the commandment to restore and to build Jerusalem unto the Messiah the Prince shall be seven weeks, and threescore and two weeks."

To Daniel was shown the long prophecy of 69 weeks that was to reach from the decree to rebuild Jerusalem to the baptism of Christ.

"Unto the Messiah the Prince." Can you imagine how Daniel must have felt as he heard these words? Wonder of wonders, this was ten thousand times better than the end of the captivity, or the rebuilding of Jerusalem! God was going to send His people the great Deliverer of whom all the prophets had spoken and for whom all Israel had yearned so long. He would make an end of sins and bring in everlasting right-eousness.

And it wouldn't be long. Not now. Only sixty-nine "weeks" of years. That was all. Just 483 years.

This was Gabriel's secret, his glorious secret.

And how wonderfully it came true!

Three kings of Medo-Persia issued commandments to re-store and build Jerusalem: Cyrus, Darius, and Artaxerxes. The last of these decrees was made in 457 B.C. Subtract 457 from 483 and what do you get? Twenty-six, of course. Any boy or girl can work that out.

But, if the last decree was given in the *spring* of 457 B.C., then 483 full years ended in the *spring* of A.D. 27. Isn't that right? Sure it's right. And what happened then?

That was the very time when Jesus Christ was baptized in the river Jordan and was anointed by the Holy Spirit as the true Messiah, God's chosen champion of righteousness, His greatest and most precious gift to a lost and hopeless world.

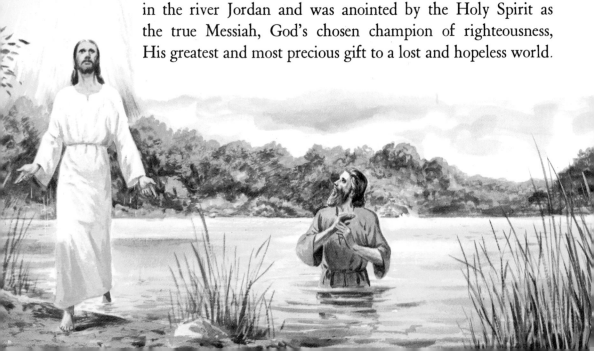

STORY 13

Daniel Sees Our Day

D ID you ever wonder why the children of Israel did not ride into the Promised Land in jeeps? Or why David didn't kill Goliath with a revolver? Or why the Wise Men from the East did not follow the Star of Bethlehem in a jet plane?

Oh, you say, because jeeps and revolvers and jet planes weren't invented in those far-off days. True, but why?

The book of Daniel tells us why. In the last chapter Gabriel lets us into another secret.

He has been telling Daniel about many things to happen in the future, clear on down to the time when "Michael . . . the great prince" shall come to rescue His people from the worst time of trouble that ever befell them. At that time of God's final victory over all evil, he says, "Many of them that sleep in the dust of the earth shall awake, some to everlasting life, and some to shame and everlasting contempt. And they that be wise shall shine as the brightness of the firmament;

71

and they that turn many to righteousness as the stars for ever and ever."

Then Gabriel says to Daniel, "But thou, O Daniel, shut up the words, and seal the book, even to the time of the end: many shall run to and fro, and knowledge shall be increased."

Strange words these! What can they mean?

"Seal the book." Which book? No doubt the book Daniel was writing at the time.

Until when? "Even to the time of the end"—the time just before God's final victory.

Then what is to happen? The book is to be unsealed. People will begin to read it, understand it, and learn of God's plans. They will begin to run to and fro telling other people the wonderful news, and there will be a great increase of knowledge all over the world.

Did you ever stop to think that this may be the reason why so many wonderful things have been invented lately— things that help people to travel quickly from place to place and make it possible for them to talk to each other over great distances?

How do you travel nowadays? On a camel, like Abraham? On a donkey, like Balaam? In a covered wagon, like the American pioneers? No, indeed. You travel by car at sixty miles an hour, or by train at one hundred miles an hour. If you wish, you can go almost anywhere by plane at 350 miles an hour, crossing oceans and continents in almost no time at all.

And how do you talk to your neighbor? Do you walk half a mile and knock on his door? Of course not. You telephone him. If he lives the other side of the country, you wire him—or telephone him, if you have the money.

And if you want to talk to a lot of people at the same time, what do you do? You get on a radio or television program. Then you can reach millions and millions all at once.

When you stop to think of it, this is a most marvelous age we are living in, with its atomic power and hydroelectric power and every other kind of power to help us do the things we want to do.

Just look around your house a moment and see what you have that great-grandfather never had, nor dreamed about. That electric washing machine, sewing machine, dishwasher, refrigerator, deepfreeze, television set, Hi-Fi set, and whatnot.

Look inside a modern hospital and see all the shiny instruments they have there to make sick people well. Nobody knew about X-ray, penicillin, sulfa drugs and things like these a hundred years ago.

Look around your school. Take another peek at all the books in the library, all the instruments in the science lab. How your grandfather would have loved all these things when he was a boy!

And they speak of knowledge. More knowledge. Increased knowledge.

How marvelous that Daniel should have seen all this, long, long, ago!

What wonderful secrets Gabriel told him!

PART II

Stories of Israel's Return

(Ezra 1:1-10:44; Nehemiah 1:1-13:31;
Haggai 1:1-2:23; Zechariah 1:1-14:21)

STORY 1

The Hour of Deliverance

WHEN Daniel was brought unharmed out of the den of lions, King Darius, you remember, sent a message to all parts of his kingdom praising the God of heaven who had so wonderfully delivered His faithful servant.

One very important person who read that message was Cyrus, commander in chief of the Medo-Persian armies, which captured Babylon.

This man, who became king upon the death of Darius, was naturally very much interested in Daniel, whom Darius had made chief of the presidents of the new kingdom.

No doubt they often talked together about the affairs of the realm. On one of these occasions Daniel may well have said to him, "Cyrus, do you know that your name is mentioned in the writings of one of the Hebrew prophets?"

"*My* name?" I can hear him saying. "Impossible!"

"But it is true," said Daniel. More than a hundred years

77

niel told Cyrus, commander in chief of the
do-Persian armies, that the prophet Isaiah,
arly a hundred and fifty years before their
ie, had named him as conqueror of Babylon.

ago, long before you were born, Isaiah wrote of you and told how you would capture Babylon."

"Let me see it for myself!" Cyrus asked, and Daniel opened the scroll of Isaiah to the forty-fifth chapter. Together they read these amazing words:

"Thus saith the Lord to his anointed, to Cyrus, whose right hand I have holden, to subdue nations before him; . . . to open before him the two leaved gates; and the gates shall not be shut; I will go before thee, and make the crooked places straight: I will break in pieces the gates of brass, and cut in sunder the bars of iron."

"The gates!" cried Cyrus. "He must have meant the gates of Babylon. They were open when we got to them, just as your prophet says."

"They were indeed," said Daniel. "But listen. 'For Jacob my servant's sake, and Israel mine elect, I have even called thee by thy name: I have surnamed thee, though thou hast not known me."

"But why?" I can hear Cyrus asking. "Why should your God think of me so long ago—long before I was born?"

"Listen again," said Daniel. The Lord "saith of Cyrus, He is my shepherd, and shall perform all my pleasure: even saying to Jerusalem, Thou shalt be built; and to the temple, Thy foundation shall be laid." "I have raised him up in righteousness, and I will direct all his ways; he shall build my city, and he shall let go my captives."

At this point it may well be that Daniel told Cyrus about that other wonderful prophecy written by Jeremiah—the one where God said His captive people would be set free after seventy years.

"How long have your people been in captivity?" Cyrus asked.

"Almost seventy years," said Daniel. "I remember when I was brought here as a boy by Nebuchadnezzar. I am too old now to return, but my people must go back. The time has come, and you have been appointed by God to deliver them."

Deeply moved, Cyrus decided to do what the God of heaven expected of him.

And so it came about that "in the first year of Cyrus king of Persia, that the word of the Lord by the mouth of Jeremiah might be fulfilled, the Lord stirred up the spirit of Cyrus king of Persia, that he made a proclamation throughout all his kingdom, and put it also in writing, saying,

"Thus saith Cyrus king of Persia, The Lord God of heaven hath given me all the kingdoms of the earth; and he hath charged me to build him an house at Jerusalem, which is in Judah.

"Who is there among you of all his people? his God be with him, and let him go up to Jerusalem, . . . and build the house of the Lord God of Israel."

The hour of deliverance had struck!

STORY 2

The Road Back

SWIFT messengers carried the good news all over the kingdom of Medo-Persia. Imagine the thrill it brought to all the Jews in captivity!

Some had been expecting something like this to happen, but many had given up all hope of seeing their homeland again.

But here came the good word that they were free to go back *now!* It was almost too good to be true.

What happened then is described in the book of Psalms:

"When the Lord turned again the captivity of Zion, we were like them that dream. Then was our mouth filled with laughter, and our tongue with singing: then said they among the heathen, the Lord hath done great things for them. The Lord hath done great things for us; whereof we are glad."

Of course everybody wasn't happy. Some were too old to go, and some were too sick. Some had new babies and the journey seemed too long and hard, while others were comfortable and didn't want to go back at all.

80

THE ROAD BACK

Suddenly every son of Abraham found himself asking the question, "Shall I go, or shall I stay?"

"I'm going," said one. "And I, and I," said others.

In no time at all whole families were packing up and moving to the place of departure. Almost fifty thousand made their way there, and what a happy crowd it was!

All were in high spirits. It was wonderful to be free at last and to know that in a little while they would be home again in their own country.

King Cyrus had been so kind to them! He had even opened his treasure house and "brought forth the vessels of the house of the Lord, which Nebuchadnezzar had brought forth out of Jerusalem and had put . . . in the house of his gods."

Best of all was the thought that God had remembered His promise and—right on time—had ended their captivity. It was so good to feel that they were in God's favor once more.

King Cyrus had put Zerubbabel (sometimes called Shesh-bazzar) in charge of the expedition. He was the grandson of King Jehoiachin, who was taken captive by Nebuchadnezzar, and might have been king of Judah himself had his grandfather been a better man. Matthew tells us that he was in the line of famous people through whom Christ came (Matthew 1:12).

Zerubbabel was made governor of Judah and Joshua, a direct descendant of Aaron, the high priest. You can imagine how busy these two men were getting everybody and everything ready for the long journey to Jerusalem.

Gradually the huge caravan was made ready. In it were 736 horses, 245 mules, 435 camels, and 6,720 asses—which is quite a lot of animals.

At long last Zerubbabel gave the signal to start. What a shout must have gone up as those ahead stepped forward and the long line of ox-drawn wagons, loaded donkeys, cows, sheep, goats, and people moved forward. I can almost see the boys and girls dancing for joy, can't you?

On to Jerusalem! was the cry upon everybody's lips. They

couldn't get there too soon. How exciting it must have been!

In the procession were "two hundred singing men and women."

How they sang, their hearts bursting with joy!

I don't know what they sang, but it may well have been that lovely psalm that says, "O give thanks unto the Lord, for he is good: for his mercy endureth for ever.

"Let the redeemed of the Lord say so, whom he hath redeemed from the land of the enemy;

"And gathered them out of the lands, from the east, and from the west, from the north, and from the south. . . .

"And he led them forth by the right way, that they might go to a city of habitation.

"Oh that men would praise the Lord for his goodness, and for his wonderful works to the children of men!"

So the caravan rolled on toward Jerusalem. In God's providence a new day had dawned for the children of Israel. A great new chance had been given them. What would they do with it?

STORY 3

Songs and Tears

SLOWLY the great caravan made its way from Babylon to Palestine. Fifty thousand people, with all those camels, horses, mules, and donkeys could not have moved very fast. But what did they care? They were free! They were going home! The long years of captivity were over at last! No wonder they sang and shouted for joy!

Just which route they took we are not told, but it could well have been the same that Abraham followed when he left Ur of the Chaldees nearly fifteen hundred years before.

At sunset each evening, as families gathered around the campfires, no doubt fathers and mothers told their children the story of that far-off day and of all that had happened since. Of Abraham's son Isaac; of Esau and Jacob; of Jacob's twelve sons who became the fathers of the twelve tribes of Israel; of the journey into Egypt and the long years of bondage there; of the great deliverance under Moses; of God's mighty miracle at the Red Sea and His many wonders in the wilderness; of

the crossing of the Jordan and the conquest of the Promised Land; of the glorious reigns of David and Solomon; of the years of wrongdoing and the final punishment.

And when these wonderful bedtime stories were ended I can hear the parents saying, "And now God in His goodness and love is giving us another chance; that is why we are going back. We must not fail Him this time."

As day followed day excitement grew. Memories of life in Babylon faded as the beloved homeland drew nearer and nearer. At last a great shout of joy went up from those in the lead. They had sighted the mountains of Judah!

Back through the whole long procession spread the glad tidings. The singers burst forth with new songs of praise while many a weary pilgrim found new strength to finish the journey.

"Are we nearly there?" I can hear some tired little boy asking his mother.

"Yes, dear, nearly there!" she says; "only a little way more."

Then came the greatest shout of all.

"Jerusalem! Jerusalem!"

They were home at last!

But it was a sad sight that met their gaze. Where the great wall had once stood nothing was left but scattered stones, as far as the eye could see. Solomon's beautiful Temple was a heap of charred ruins. So, too, was the royal palace and all the fine homes and stores that some of the returning captives remembered so well. All were gone. Only a few poor houses remained.

So this was Jerusalem! The children and young people, who had never seen it before, must have been very disappointed.

SONGS AND TEARS

Some may well have said, "Imagine coming such a long way just for this!"

Of course the dreadful ruins were no surprise to the two leaders, Zerubbabel and Joshua the high priest. They knew all along what they would find. And now—the very first thing —they set to work to rebuild the altar that had once stood in the Temple court. This done, they offered burnt offerings upon it, the first so offered in many, many years.

I suppose the whole fifty thousand people, men, women, and children, crowded as near as they could to take part in that first service of thanksgiving on their return. They stood on parts of broken columns, smashed arches, upturned stones— anywhere—just so they could get close enough to see and hear what was going on. And as the smoke of the sacrifice rose into the evening sky all heads bowed in thankfulness to God for delivering them from Babylon and bringing them safely home again.

In the days that followed, the people scattered over the countryside looking for good farmland and places where they could build their homes.

Meanwhile Zerubbabel sent messengers to Tyre and Sidon to buy cedar trees, which were to be sent by sea to Joppa, for the rebuilding of the Temple. At the same time he ordered stonemasons to begin clearing the site.

It wasn't easy to get started, especially as the whole city had lain in ruins for the best part of seventy years. But so well did everybody work that within seven months Zerubbabel was ready to lay the foundations of the new building.

What a ceremony that was! Once more the people crowded round. Priests and Levites, all dressed in their robes, came with trumpets and cymbals. "And they sang together by course in praising and giving thanks unto the Lord; because he is good, for his mercy endureth for ever toward Israel."

How happy they were!

"And all the people shouted with a great shout, when they praised the Lord, because the foundation of the house of the Lord was laid."

Then the strangest thing happened. In the midst of the singing a sound of wailing was heard. While all the young people were shouting for joy, all the old people were crying out loud, with tears running down their cheeks. "So that the people could not discern the noise of the shout of joy from the noise of the weeping . . . : for the people shouted with a great shout, and the noise was heard afar off."

The trouble was, of course, that the old men, "the chief of the fathers, who were ancient men," remembered the old days and the glory of Solomon's Temple, and this one seemed so small, so poor, by comparison. So they wept; and songs and tears were mingled on this day of the new beginning.

STORY 4

More Trouble

WHILE some were glad and some were sad over the rebuilding of the Temple there were other people not far away who were very much upset by what was going on in Jerusalem. They didn't like it a bit.

These people were the grandchildren—or great-grandchildren—of the strangers who had been brought into Palestine by the Assyrian kings when Israel had first been taken away into captivity. Known as Samaritans, they had lived here so long now that they felt the country belonged to them. That's why the sudden return of fifty thousand Jewish refugees worried them so much. They were afraid of what might happen to them and their property if the Jews should become strong again as they had been under David, Solomon, and Hezekiah.

One day a group of these people came to Zerubbabel and offered to help rebuild the Temple. Of course they planned to hinder rather than help, and Zerubbabel quickly saw through their little plot.

"No, thank you," he said to them. "We will build this house of God ourselves." And he sent them about their business. This was the beginning of all the trouble between the Jews and the Samaritans.

Greatly annoyed, these men "hired counsellors" to work against the Jews "to frustrate their purpose, all the days of Cyrus king of Persia, even until the reign of Darius king of Persia."

They could not do much damage during the reign of Cyrus. That great king had learned too much of God's purposes for Israel from the prophet Daniel to be swayed by evil reports from their enemies. But after Cyrus was dead and another king had taken his place things were different.

Now these enemies sent another letter, a copy of which is to be found in the fourth chapter of the book of Ezra. It ran like this:

"Be it known unto the king, that the Jews which came up from thee to us are come unto Jerusalem, building the rebellious and the bad city, and have set up the walls thereof, and joined the foundations.

"Be it known now unto the king, that, if this city be builded, and the walls set up again, then will they not pay toll, tribute, and custom. . . .

"Now . . . therefore have we sent and certified the king; that search may be made in the book of the records of thy fathers: so shalt thou find in the . . . records, and know that this city is a rebellious city, and hurtful unto kings and provinces, and that they have moved sedition within the same of old time: for which cause was this city destroyed."

The letter did its work. The king looked up the records and found evidence enough that Jerusalem had given plenty of trouble to the kings of Babylon and Assyria. He may even have run across the story of Sennacherib's defeat, when that famous king lost 185,000 men in a single night outside the walls of Jerusalem.

In his reply to Rehum and his friends the king told how he had had the records searched and had found that Jerusalem had indeed been a hotbed of rebellion in days gone by. Therefore, he ordered, the rebuilding of the city must stop at once.

Delighted with the success of their plan, Rehum and his friends hurried to Jerusalem with many armed men. Backed by the king's letter, they made the builders put down their tools.

"Then ceased the work of the house of God . . . at Jerusalem."

What a sad moment that must have been!

After coming so far, and doing so much, it must have been heartbreaking to be told to stop.

What could it mean? The people wondered. Had there been a mistake? Should they have stayed in Babylon? Had God forsaken them?

STORY 5

Cheer Up! Be Strong!

THOSE were dark days. Even Zerubbabel and Joshua were discouraged. They couldn't understand why God had let this happen. It seemed too bad that after the wonderful deliverance from Babylon, when the people were so eager to rebuild the Temple, the work should have to stop.

In their disappointment many of the people began to build nice houses for themselves. They argued that work on the Temple had been started too soon; that God's time for rebuilding it hadn't come yet.

But there had been no mistake. This setback was just a test of their faith and courage. God had not forsaken them. Indeed He was very near, watching everything they did. One day He sent the prophet Haggai to see Zerubbabel and Joshua.

Speaking in the name of God, Haggai said to the governor: "This people say, The time is not come, the time that the Lord's house should be built"; but, "Is it time for you, O ye, to dwell in your cieled houses, and this house lie waste?

CHEER UP! BE STRONG!

"Now therefore thus saith the Lord of hosts; Consider your ways.

"Ye have sown much, and bring in little; ye eat, but ye have not enough; ye drink, but ye are not filled with drink; ye clothe you, but there is none warm; and he that earneth wages earneth wages to put it into a bag with holes.

"Thus saith the Lord of hosts; Consider your ways.

"Go up to the mountain, and bring wood, and build the house; and I will take pleasure in it, and I will be glorified, saith the Lord."

Zerubbabel and Joshua listened carefully. They recognized the voice of God speaking through His prophet. Everything Haggai had said was true. From the moment the people had stopped building the Temple nobody had been happy. They had started to work for themselves, but there had been no blessing in it. Any money they had earned had disappeared just as if they had put it into a bag full of holes.

Haggai was right. It was time to consider their ways; time to return to God; time to complete their unfinished task.

The two leaders talked the matter over together and decided to obey "the voice of the Lord their God, and the words of Haggai the prophet." As they did so new courage came into their hearts, and they began to talk courage to the people.

"And the Lord stirred up the spirit of Zerubbabel . . . and the spirit of Joshua . . . and the spirit of all the remnant of the people; and they came and did work in the house of the Lord of hosts, their God."

From far and near they came, and soon the sound of hammers, the chink of iron on stone, and the laughter and shouts of happy builders were heard again around the Temple.

Now it was that God sent another message to the two leaders—one of the most wonderful to be found in all the Bible. Because they had obeyed His voice, He let them know one of His great secrets, which before then He dared not reveal.

They were not to be sad because this new Temple was not nearly so beautiful as the one Solomon had built. They were to build it just the same. And He would bless them marvelously.

"Be strong, O Zerubbabel, saith the Lord; and be strong, O Joshua . . . ; and be strong, all ye people of the land, . . . and work: for I am with you, saith the Lord of hosts:

"According to the word that I covenanted with you when ye came out of Egypt, so my spirit remaineth among you: fear ye not."

God had not forgotten His promises—not even those made fifteen hundred years before! His Spirit remained with His people still, despite all their waywardness and sin.

Yet this was not all. Something far, far better was in store.

"Yet once, it is a little while, and I will shake the heavens, and the earth, and the sea, and the dry land; and I will shake all nations, and the desire of all nations shall come: and I will fill this house with glory, saith the Lord of hosts. . . . The glory of this latter house shall be greater than of the former . . . : and in this place will I give peace."

Thus God drew back the curtain of the future and let Zerubbabel and Joshua see the coming of Jesus, the Messiah, the "desire of all nations." He would come to this very place, and His presence would fill it with glory.

And it would not be long now. Not very long. Just "a little while," said Haggai. Less than five hundred years; and what is that to God?

STORY 6

A Mountain Becomes a Plain

TO BRING still more courage to Zerubbabel God sent a second prophet to him with another cheering message. Just when the governor's problems had piled up in front of him like a great mountain, God told him, through the prophet Zechariah, that they would suddenly vanish.

And it wouldn't be because of anything Zerubbabel did himself. He wouldn't have to organize an army, or buy the king's favor with money. No, said Zechariah. Help would come "not by might, nor by power, but by my spirit, saith the Lord of hosts."

Then, said the prophet, as though he were talking to all the governor's troubles: "Who art thou, O great mountain? before Zerubbabel thou shalt become a plain."

As for the building of the Temple, there was no need for him to worry. "The hands of Zerubbabel have laid the foundation of this house; his hands shall also finish it."

To those who had been finding fault with what the gover-

96

nor had done, the prophet said, "Who hath despised the day of small things? for they shall rejoice, and shall see the plummet in the hand of Zerubbabel."

A plummet is a piece of metal or stone on a string, which a builder uses to see that his walls are straight. All who had laughed at Zerubbabel would see him with such a tool in his hands testing the finished walls of the Temple. Then it would be his turn to laugh at them.

So it was that God sought to cheer this good man who had been trying to do his best under very great difficulties.

And what happened?

Zerubbabel and Joshua took up their task again, "And with them were the prophets of God helping them."

Hardly had they started, however, when more trouble arose. The mountain seemed to get bigger than ever.

Tatnai, who had taken the place of Rehum, came with a company of soldiers and asked, "Who hath commanded you to build this house, and to make up this wall? . . . What are the names of the men that make this building?"

Patiently Zerubbabel explained: "We are the servants of the God of heaven and earth, and build the house that was builded these many years ago, which a great king of Israel builded and set up."

Then he told how, because of their sins, God had allowed His people to be carried into captivity by Nebuchadnezzar, but that seventy years later "king Cyrus made a decree to build this house of God." We have been building it ever since, he added, "and yet it is not finished."

Tatnai said he would have to send a report to King Darius and see what he would have to say. Fortunately his letter was written in a more kindly tone than the one Rehum had sent years before. He merely asked that search be made in the imperial records to see whether King Cyrus ever made such a decree as Zerubbabel had spoken of.

Of course, when King Darius had the records examined he found everything in order. King Cyrus *had* released the Jewish captives and *had* ordered them to rebuild their Temple. So he sent this message to Tatnai:

"Let the work of this house of God alone; let the governor of the Jews and the elders of the Jews build this house of God in his place."

Then, of all things, he ordered Tatnai to take part of the king's tribute money and give it to the Jews to help pay the expenses of their building! In addition, he said that young bullocks, rams and lambs, also wheat, salt, wine and oil, were to be provided for the burnt offerings of the God of heaven at Jerusalem. "And let it be given them day by day without fail," he said.

Tatnai was one surprised man when he received this order from King Darius, and he hurried to Jerusalem to assure Zerubbabel that he would do as he had been told.

"And the elders of the Jews builded, and they prospered through the prophesying of Haggai the prophet and Zechariah the son of Iddo. And they builded, and finished it, according to the commandment of the God of Israel, and according to the commandment of Cyrus, and Darius, and Artaxerxes king of Persia.

"And this house was finished on the third day of the month Adar, which was in the sixth year of the reign of Darius the king."

So the mountain became a plain, even as God had said.

STORY 7

Why Ezra Blushed

ALL THE Jews who lived in Babylon—or Medo-Persia— did not go back to Jerusalem when King Cyrus made his famous decree giving them permission to do so. Many stayed on even after the second decree, given by Darius. Some were still there when King Artaxerxes made his decree in the year 457 B.C.

Among these was a man named Ezra, "a ready scribe in the law of Moses" who could trace his family tree clear back to Aaron.

Feeling the pull of his homeland, and eager to see what had been done there since the first freed captives returned, Ezra sought the king's permission to lead a company of his friends to Jerusalem.

Graciously the king agreed, at the same time giving Ezra a very precious document.

"Artaxerxes, king of kings, unto Ezra the priest," it began. "I make a decree, that all they of the people of Israel, and of

100

his priests and Levites, in my realm, which are minded of their own freewill to go up to Jerusalem, go with thee."

This decree also permitted Ezra to take with him all the silver and gold he could collect to help the work of God in Jerusalem, and gave him authority to appoint magistrates and judges with full power to punish offenders with imprisonment or death. No Jew had had such power since the Babylonians took over the country.

Compared with the fifty thousand who returned with Zerubbabel, Ezra's party was very small. Fewer than two thousand men joined it, besides women and children, of course.

Because they were carrying so much money, some in the company were afraid of being attacked by bandits on the way, but Ezra "was ashamed to require of the king a band of soldiers and horsemen to help . . . against the enemy in the way:" because he had "spoken unto the king, saying, The hand of our God is upon all them for good that seek him."

So they fasted and prayed and asked God to look after them. This He did, and after a journey of four months they arrived safely at Jerusalem with all their money quite safe.

It was a great day when they rode at last into the Holy City. Proudly and happily they handed over the gold and silver

to the priests in charge of the Temple. But their joy did not last long.

Ezra had not been in Jerusalem more than a few days when he heard something that made him blush for shame.

The princes broke the sad news to him. "The people of Israel, and the priests, and the Levites," they said, "have not separated themselves from the people of the lands. . . . For they have taken of their daughters for themselves, and for their sons."

Ezra was astonished. This was one of the things God had told His people not to do. On no account were the young men to marry girls who did not believe in Him. This had been Solomon's great sin, which had brought so much sorrow upon Israel. Now they were doing it again—only a few short years after God had set them free.

That evening, says Ezra, "I fell upon my knees, and spread out my hands unto the Lord my God, and said, O my God, I am ashamed and blush to lift up my face to thee, my God: for our iniquities are increased over our head, and our trespass is grown up unto the heavens."

He thanked God for leading the kings of Persia to show mercy to His people in setting them free and letting them rebuild the Temple.

"And now, O our God," he cried, "what shall we say after this? . . . After all that is come upon us for our evil deeds, and for our great trespass, seeing that thou our God hast punished us less than our iniquities deserve, and hast given us such deliverance as this;

WHY EZRA BLUSHED

"Should we again break thy commandments, and join in affinity with the people of these abominations? wouldest not thou be angry with us till thou hadst consumed us, so that there should be no remnant nor escaping?"

So he pleaded for God's forgiveness; for one more chance to do right.

Then he called all Israel together and told them what was on his heart. Earnestly he begged them to undo the wrong they had done while yet there was time.

That was a very sad meeting. Not only were many people worried because they did not know what to do with the heathen wives they had married, but everyone was cold, wet, and miserable, because it was raining heavily at the time.

At last, with one voice the people said, "As thou hast said, so must we do."

Of course it wasn't possible to break up so many marriages overnight; and there were the children to be thought of, too. It took days and weeks to straighten things out properly. A special court was set up to try all the cases, and three months passed before the task was finished.

It had to be done, of course, or Israel would soon have slipped back into idolatry again; but what a lot of sad good-bys there must have been!

STORY 8

The King's Cupbearer

ABOUT twelve years after this a man by the name of Hanani traveled from Jerusalem to Shushan, a city near the Persian Gulf where the king had one of his palaces. Just why he went on so long a journey nobody knows, but when he got there Nehemiah, the king's cupbearer, sent for him.

"What news is there from Jerusalem?" asked Nehemiah, who also was a Jew. "How are the people getting along? What has happened to Ezra and those who went back with him? Have they rebuilt the city walls yet?"

There were no newspapers in those days, no radio or television, so about the only way one could get news of other parts of the world was by asking travelers such as Hanani.

Hanani's report was not a cheerful one. From what he had seen, the people who had returned from captivity were "in great affliction and reproach." Things were not going well. True, the Temple had been rebuilt, and services were being held in it, but as for the city wall, it was still largely broken down and the gates burned with fire just as they had been for many, many years.

On hearing this Nehemiah felt very sad. For several days he mourned "and fasted, and prayed before the God of heaven."

"I beseech thee, O Lord God of heaven," he cried; "the great and terrible God, that keepeth covenant and mercy for them that love him and observe his commandments: let thine ear now be attentive, and thine eyes open, that thou mayest hear the prayer of thy servant, which I pray before thee now, day and night, for the children of Israel."

As he prayed the thought came to him that perhaps he should go to Jerusalem and do what needed to be done there. But how could he leave his job? Was he not the king's cupbearer?

So he prayed that if God wanted him to go to Jerusalem He would "grant him mercy in the sight of this man"—King Artaxerxes.

Soon after this, as he was waiting on the king, the whole matter came up in a most unexpected way.

As the king's cupbearer, Nehemiah was expected to be always smiling and cheerful, but this particular day he was

so upset by the news he had heard from Jerusalem that he felt more like crying than laughing.

The king noticed that he was not as happy as usual.

"What's the matter?" he asked. "Are you sick?"

"No, my lord," replied Nehemiah.

"Then why do you look so sad? If you are not sick, this is nothing else but sorrow of heart."

At this Nehemiah became very frightened, for he knew only too well that the king hated to have sad-faced people about him.

"Your Majesty," he said with deep respect. "Why should my face not be sad when the city where my fathers are buried is all broken down?"

"Have you a request to make?" asked the king kindly.

Sending up a silent prayer to God, Nehemiah replied, "If it please the king, send me to Judah, to the city where my fathers are buried, that I may build it."

"How long would this journey take?" asked the king. "When will you return?"

Nehemiah named the time he thought it would take and, to his great joy, the king agreed to let him go. Not only so, but he sent with him "captains of the army and horsemen" to see him safely to Jerusalem. He also gave him a written order to the "keeper of the king's forest" to provide all the wood he might need for whatever rebuilding he planned to do.

Thus Nehemiah's prayer was answered in a very wonderful way; and the king's cupbearer—to his own great surprise—was soon on his way to the city of his dreams.

107

When the king saw the downcast face of Nehemiah, his cupbearer, he granted his request that he might return to the land of his fathers to rebuild the walls of Jerusalem.

STORY 9

Secret Journey

WHEN Nehemiah rode into Jerusalem with his escort of Persian captains and cavalrymen, a good many people must have wondered who he was and why he had come. Perhaps they thought he was just another tax collector, or maybe a wealthy merchant who had hired these soldiers to guard him on his journey.

Whatever they may have thought, Nehemiah did not satisfy their curiosity. He wanted to see a few things for himself before telling anybody why he had come.

Knowing that people would be suspicious if he were to look around the city by day, he decided to make his inspection by night, and this is how he tells the story:

"I arose in the night, I and some few men with me; neither told I any man what my God had put in my heart to do at Jerusalem. . . . And I went out by night by the gate of the valley, even before the dragon well, and to the dung port, and viewed the walls of Jerusalem, which were

108

broken down, and the gates thereof were consumed with fire.

"Then I went on to the gate of the fountain, and to the king's pool."

Here he had to dismount, for "there was no place for the beast that was under me to pass.

"Then went I up in the night by the brook, and viewed the wall, and turned back, and entered by the gate of the valley, and so returned."

It must have been an eerie journey as, in the dim moonlight, the little group of men made their way between huge boulders, scattered stones, and heaps of rubbish overgrown with moss and weeds. Many times they must have thought of the days of Israel's glory when David and Solomon built Jerusalem and made it known and honored throughout the world.

Nehemiah was shocked by what he saw. Such utter ruin! Such awful desolation! It seemed hard to believe that almost ninety years after the first captives had returned in the reign of Cyrus there should still be all this mess and so little done to rebuild the walls of the city. Surely God could not be pleased to see the capital of Israel in such a sorry state!

Next day he went to see the rulers of the city.

Whether he told them of his secret journey of the night before the Bible does not say, but we do know that he talked eagerly about the need to rebuild the walls.

"Ye see the distress that we are in," he said to them, "how Jerusalem lieth waste, and the gates thereof are burned with fire: come, and let us build up the wall of Jerusalem, that we be no more a reproach."

Some no doubt smiled at the zeal of this newcomer; others shrugged their shoulders and asked what they could do about it. Still others simply said, "Where's the money?"

But Nehemiah was not one to be put off with excuses. He had an answer for every objection. His motto was, It can be done! And he kept on talking courage until the rulers began to think he might be right after all.

Of course he told about his position in the court of Arta-xerxes and of the king's favors, including the important letter to the keeper of the king's forest ordering him to supply all the wood that might be needed.

Surely, he pleaded, this must be the time to act; it must be God's hour of opportunity. Then, with shining eyes and face aglow he cried, "Let us arise and build!"

The rulers were convinced. They liked this man who had suddenly come among them. He had something. Clearly, he was a born leader. Maybe he could help them do what they had known for a long time should be done. They caught his spirit. Soon they were talking courage too. "So they strengthened their hands for this good work."

STORY 10

Working Together

A S WORD spread that the walls of Jerusalem were going to be rebuilt at last, the dead city came to life. New hope filled every heart.

Ever since the first captives had returned from Babylon, people had talked about doing the job, but always it had been put off to some other time. It would take too long; there was so much else to do first; and, anyway, there was no money.

Now a man had come among them saying, "It can be done!" and, "Let's do it now!" And everybody caught his spirit and yearned to spring into action.

As Nehemiah went about the city he kept on talking courage to everyone he met, whether priest, noble, ruler, or one of "the rest that did the work." To every doubter he would say, "Of course we can do it. You'll see. God is with us. He will help us. If everybody does his best we'll have this wall up in no time."

No doubt people smiled at him, but all the same they

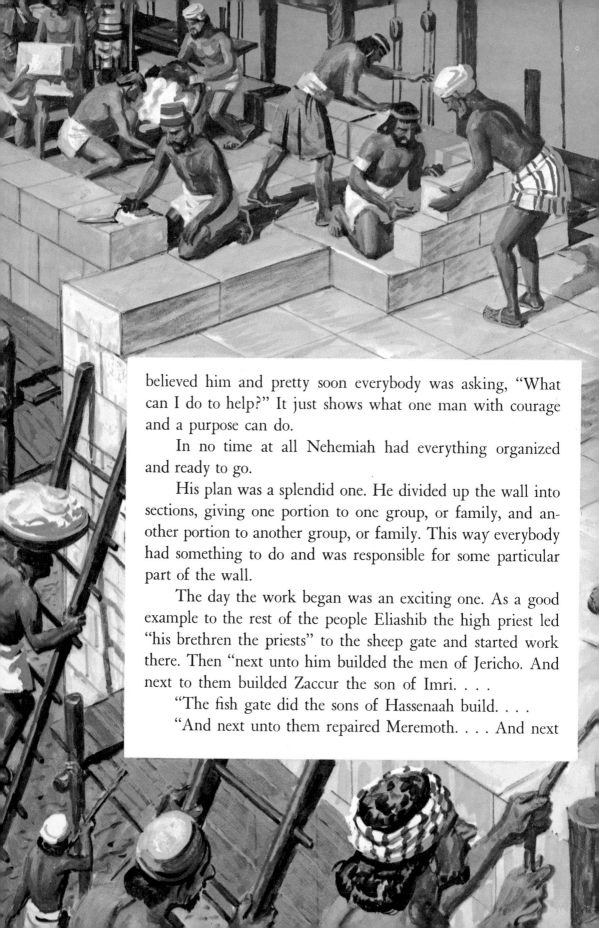

believed him and pretty soon everybody was asking, "What can I do to help?" It just shows what one man with courage and a purpose can do.

In no time at all Nehemiah had everything organized and ready to go.

His plan was a splendid one. He divided up the wall into sections, giving one portion to one group, or family, and another portion to another group, or family. This way everybody had something to do and was responsible for some particular part of the wall.

The day the work began was an exciting one. As a good example to the rest of the people Eliashib the high priest led "his brethren the priests" to the sheep gate and started work there. Then "next unto him builded the men of Jericho. And next to them builded Zaccur the son of Imri. . . .

"The fish gate did the sons of Hassenaah build. . . .

"And next unto them repaired Meremoth. . . . And next

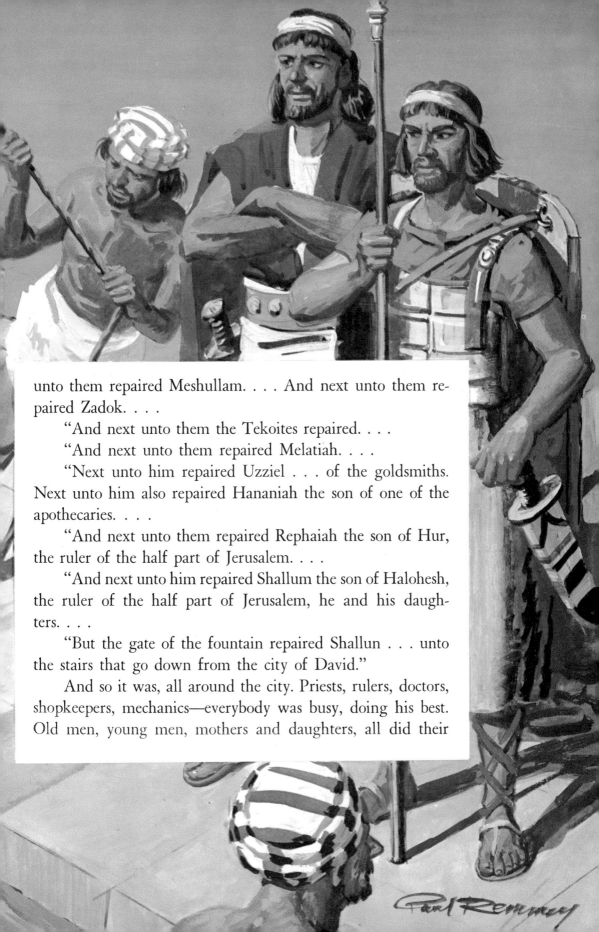

unto them repaired Meshullam. . . . And next unto them repaired Zadok. . . .

"And next unto them the Tekoites repaired. . . .

"And next unto them repaired Melatiah. . . .

"Next unto him repaired Uzziel . . . of the goldsmiths. Next unto him also repaired Hananiah the son of one of the apothecaries. . . .

"And next unto them repaired Rephaiah the son of Hur, the ruler of the half part of Jerusalem. . . .

"And next unto him repaired Shallum the son of Halohesh, the ruler of the half part of Jerusalem, he and his daughters. . . .

"But the gate of the fountain repaired Shallun . . . unto the stairs that go down from the city of David."

And so it was, all around the city. Priests, rulers, doctors, shopkeepers, mechanics—everybody was busy, doing his best. Old men, young men, mothers and daughters, all did their

part. And I am sure that all the boys and girls were fetching
and carrying and doing all they could to help.

Some worked harder than others. It is said of "Barucn
the son of Zabbai" that he "*earnestly* repaired" his piece of
the wall; but a few—as usual—refused to do anything. Of the
Tekoites the record says, "Their nobles put not their necks to
the work of their Lord." In other words, they were slackers.

But with so many people working so happily and eagerly
it wasn't long before the wall began to take shape. Some mixed
mortar, others lifted stones, and still others saw to it that they
were set in the right place. Meanwhile the less skilled people
brought more and more material of one kind and another to
the building sites.

No doubt each group had half an eye on the next group
to see how fast it was getting along; and I wouldn't be surprised if there was quite a little competition to see which
group could build the most wall in a day. I am sure, too, that
they helped each other when things got difficult, as perhaps
when one of the larger stones was too big for one family to
move.

As for Nehemiah, he was hurrying here and there, radi-
ating courage, cheering everybody on.

Not in many, many years had the people of Jerusalem
been so busy or so happy. And the most wonderful thing about
it all was the fact that the job that couldn't be done was being
done, right before their eyes.

The walls of the city were going up at last!

STORY 11

The Plain of Ono

IT'S A strange thing, but whenever anybody tries to do some great work for God somebody else tries to stop it.

So it was with the building of the walls of Jerusalem. No sooner had Nehemiah got all the people working on the job than Sanballat, Tobiah, and Geshem started to fuss about it.

To begin with, they didn't like Nehemiah. When they heard of his arrival "it grieved them exceedingly that there was come a man to seek the welfare of the children of Israel." Then, when the building began, they stood around laughing and scoffing.

"What do these feeble Jews?" mocked Sanballat. "Will they fortify themselves? . . . will they revive the stones out of the heaps of the rubbish which are burned?"

"Pshaw," sneered Tobiah, "a fox could push it over!"

This did not bother Nehemiah. He just went on building. However, when about half the wall was finished, news reached him that Sanballat, Tobiah, and Geshem were gathering an army to attack the city and knock the wall down again. Friendly Jews out in the country sent word that these enemies planned to creep up through the piles of rubbish that were not yet cleared away and pounce on the builders "and slay them, and cause the work to cease."

Nehemiah, unafraid, acted at once. He ordered everybody to drop their building tools and stand on the wall with swords, spears, and bows ready to meet the attackers. At the same time he passed this cheering message from one to another all around the city: "Be not ye afraid of them: remember the Lord, which is great and terrible, and fight for your brethren, your sons, and your daughters, your wives, and your houses."

Fortunately there was no need to fight. When Sanballat and his men, creeping up to attack the city, saw the half-built wall lined with armed men, they took fright and fled.

From that moment on, however, Nehemiah never felt quite safe. At any moment the ruffians might return. So he gave orders that half the people should go on with the building while

the other half stood guard. As an extra safeguard every builder carried his sword by his side as he worked.

"So we laboured in the work," the record reads: "and half of them held the spears from the rising of the morning till the stars appeared."

All night long, too, a careful watch was kept. Some, including Nehemiah, never took off their clothes, night or day, except "that every one put them off for washing."

With such inspiring leadership it's no wonder the work went on quickly. Day by day the wall rose higher and higher. More and more sections were joined, closing up the holes in between. What shouts of joy there must have been as the last stones were laid and family after family climbed to the top and walked along the completed wall!

One day, when the whole city was enclosed, and nothing was left to be done but hang the gates on their hinges, who should turn up but some of Sanballat's men.

"Come, let us meet together in some one of the villages in the plain of Ono," was the message they brought from their master.

Nehemiah was not that easily taken in. He knew they planned to do him harm. So he sent back this word: "I am doing a great work, so that I cannot come down: why should the work cease, whilst I leave it, and come down to you?"

Four times Sanballat sent his messengers asking Nehemiah to come down to the plain of Ono, and four times this gallant leader gave him the same answer: No, I can't do it! And that is what you should say when you are tempted to do

wrong or to leave some duty God has asked you to perform.

When Sanballat's messengers came the fifth time they brought a very nasty message. It suggested that the Jews were planning to rebel against the king of Medo-Persia and that was why they had rebuilt the wall. If Nehemiah would not come to see Sanballat, then this report would be sent to the king.

"It isn't true," replied Nehemiah. "You are making it all up yourself." And still he refused to leave his work. Then he turned to God and cried, "Now therefore, O God, strengthen my hands."

Now someone suggested that his life was in danger; that the enemy had men inside the city seeking to kill him. He had better hide in the Temple for safety.

"Should such a man as I flee?" retorted this noble leader, "and who is there, that, being as I am, would go into the temple to save his life? I will not go in."

And he didn't. Bravely he carried on with the task he had come to Jerusalem to do.

At last the wall was finished and the gates were all set in place.

How long had it taken to do this great work that some had said was impossible? You'd never guess. Just fifty-two days! Less than two months! And all because one man had vision, faith, and courage.

What a man was the king's cupbearer!

STORY 12

Great Joy in Jerusalem

WHEN the last stone had been laid and the last gate hung in place, Nehemiah laid plans for the dedication of the wall.

Invitations were sent to the people in all the nearby villages. In particular the Levites and "the sons of the singers" were asked to come. Nehemiah wanted everybody who could sing, or play a musical instrument, to be there, for it was going to be a day of great rejoicing.

And what a day it was! Everybody was there. Men, women, and children from far and near poured into the city. With pride and joy they gazed up at the newly built wall, gaping in wonder at the fine new gates.

Anyone who had helped in the building was glad for every hour he had worked and every stone he had lifted.

Then the procession began. Priests and Levites walked ahead "and purified the people, and the gates, and the wall." After them went the princes of Judah and "two great companies of them that gave thanks." They went up "by the stairs of the city of David" and one went to the right and the other to the left on the top of the wall, which was thronged with sight-seers.

When all were in their right places the priests lifted their trumpets and blew a triumphant blast, which echoed and re-echoed from the surrounding hills. Then the singers began. And how they sang!

> "O give thanks unto the Lord,
>   For He is good:
>   For His mercy endureth for ever!"

Give thanks! Give thanks! Give thanks!

Soon everybody was singing. The top of the wall was crowded with singing men, singing women, singing children. And so loud did they sing that strangers far down the valley heard the sound and looked up to see the wonderful sight.

How happy everybody was that day! "For God had made them rejoice with great joy: the wives also and the children rejoiced: so that the joy of Jerusalem was heard even afar off."

It was about this time, after the wall had been finished, that Nehemiah called all the people to meet him near the water gate. They came "as one man" and soon every inch of space was filled. Everybody was eager to hear his hero speak.

To their surprise they saw that a tall wooden pulpit had been built near the gate and they supposed that Nehemiah planned to talk to them. But it was not Nehemiah who spoke this time, but Ezra—dear old Ezra—the man who had led thousands of Jews back to Jerusalem several years before.

During all the bustle and excitement of the building, the aging scribe had been out of sight, busy no doubt with his books and his Temple duties. But now he was back and everybody was glad to see him.

In his hand he held a scroll containing the sacred book of the law. "And when he opened it, all the people stood up."

It was not the whole Bible that he held, of course, for the New Testament, and much of the Old Testament, was not written at that time. Probably all he had was a volume containing the five books of Moses, from Genesis to Deuteronomy, but oh how precious it was! All written by hand, it was one of very few copies in existence.

Many of the people in the crowd had never heard this book read before. Others could not understand it because the language was different. They had grown up in Medo-Persia and the Hebrew that Moses used was beyond them. However, whether they understood it or not, they stood respectfully and paid attention.

On and on the old man read, "from the morning until midday." Then some of the other priests took over and "read in the book in the law of God distinctly, and gave the sense, and caused them to understand the reading."

123

As the people listened they became very sad. Gradually it dawned upon them what glorious plans God had had for Israel and how terribly disappointed He must be in them. Even now, after all His mercies, they were not living up to the high standards He had set for them. Some began to weep. Soon all were weeping.

At this Nehemiah went into the pulpit and tried to cheer their hearts. This was not a day for mourning, he said, "for this day is holy unto our Lord: neither be ye sorry; for the joy of the Lord is your strength." They had done a great work for God. He was pleased with them; if they lived aright He would continue to bless them.

Just like Nehemiah! Always trying to bring cheer and courage to people.

Soon smiles came back on the sad, gloomy faces. The meeting broke up, and the people went away to eat. Sorrow turned to joy "and there was very great gladness" in Jerusalem.

STORY 13

Broken Promises

THE READING of the Word of God went on day after day. As a result there came a great revival of godliness. In their hearts the people wanted to be good and please the Lord. Three hours a day they listened as Ezra and other priests read to them; and three hours a day they confessed their sins "and worshipped the Lord their God."

One day one of the leaders cried, "Stand up and bless the Lord your God for ever and ever."

They stood. Then with bowed heads they joined in this beautiful prayer:

"Blessed be thy glorious name, which is exalted above all blessing and praise.

"Thou, even thou, art Lord alone; thou hast made heaven, the heaven of heavens, with all their host, the earth, and all things that are therein, the seas, and all that is therein, and thou preservest them all; and the host of heaven worshippeth thee."

Solemnly and gratefully they thanked God for all He had done for His people from the day He called Abraham out of Ur of the Chaldees to the present time. For the Exodus from Egypt; for the "laws of truth" given on Sinai; for bread from heaven; for victories in Canaan; and finally for deliverance from captivity. In all this, they said, "Thou hast done right, but we have done wickedly."

To prove they really meant to be good from now on they drew up an agreement and signed it. Princes, priests, and people "entered . . . into an oath, to walk in God's law."

In this document they agreed, among other things,

1. That they would not let their girls marry heathen boys; or their boys marry heathen girls.

2. That they would not buy anything on the Sabbath.

3. That they would pay so much a year to help keep up the Temple services.

4. That they would pay their tithe to the priests and Levites.

Nehemiah was the first to sign the document. Then all

the other leaders signed it. What a solemn agreement it was!

With the people thus pledged to do right, and the wall built, Nehemiah felt it was a good time to go back to Medo-Persia and report to the king, as he had promised to do.

How long he stayed there we do not know. Certainly he must have been away from Jerusalem many months, possibly years.

At last he got permission from the king to return; and it was a good thing he did.

Already—so soon!—princes, priests, and people had forgotten the pledge they had made. Eliashib, the high priest, had actually allowed Tobiah, one of Israel's worst enemies, to move into the tithe room of the Temple and live there!

Nehemiah was furious. "It grieved me sore," he says: "therefore I cast forth all the household stuff of Tobiah out of the chamber."

But Eliashib had done something much worse. He had allowed his son to marry the daughter of Sanballat, of all people! Nehemiah was so disgusted that he says, "I chased him from me."

As Nehemiah continued his inquiries he found that the people had not kept their promise to pay their tithe, with the result that the Levites were starving. He soon changed that.

Then he noticed that on the Sabbath, which was supposed to be a holy day, the people were acting just as though it were an ordinary weekday. They were buying and selling, harvesting and traveling, seemingly without a thought that this was God's day.

127

Fearlessly he went to the princes and told them what he thought. "What evil thing is this that ye do, and profane the sabbath day?" he stormed. "Did not your fathers thus, and did not our God bring all this evil upon us, and upon this city? yet ye bring more wrath upon Israel by profaning the sabbath."

Always a man of action, Nehemiah determined to put a stop to this wrongdoing at once. So he set some of his own faithful servants at every gate, with orders to close them at sunset every Friday evening and not to open them till after the Sabbath.

He had built these gates as a protection against Israel's enemies; now he shut them to help his people remember the Sabbath day to keep it holy.

So Nehemiah, the king's cupbearer, tried his best to bring Israel back to God; to keep them in the way of truth and righteousness; to save them from further punishment. Alas, but few heeded his counsel, and the sad story of broken promises went on and on down the years.

PART III

Stories of Queen Esther

(ESTHER 1:1-10:3)

STORY 1

A Star Is Born

I F YOU had lived in Shushan, capital of Medo-Persia, a little less than twenty-five hundred years ago, you might have run across a very sad little girl.

Her name was Hadassah, the Hebrew name for Myrtle. She was very pretty, but oh, so unhappy! You see, her daddy had been dead for some time, and now her mamma had died too, and she was all alone in the world.

Of course, in those hard, cruel times, it was nothing new for a little girl to be left an orphan, but that didn't help poor Hadassah. All she could think of was that she had nobody to love her, nobody that is, except maybe her big cousin Mordecai. He was much older than she, and married, with a home of his own and a job at the royal palace. She might be able to stay with him, if he would let her, if he cared enough for her.

Fortunately Mordecai did care. Gladly he took poor little Hadassah into his home and adopted her as his own daughter. Then he gave her a Persian name, "Esther," which means "a

131

Mordecai loved his little orphan cousin Hadassah and cared for her in his own home, not knowing that someday as the lovely Queen Esther she would deliver the Jews.

star." You can recognize it in the word "asteroid," which is a very little star, and in "aster," the lovely starlike flower. In Babylon the morning and evening stars were worshiped as gods under the name "Ishtar."

What a bright little star Esther proved to be! "Fair and beautiful," she was the light of Mordecai's home and the pride and joy of his heart. You can imagine how glad he was in the evenings, when he returned from the palace, to find her waiting for him with open arms. And night after night you may be sure he told her the dear old stories of God's wonderful love for His people, and how He had watched over them, in good times and bad, for hundreds and hundreds of years.

So Esther grew up to love and honor God. She learned to pray to Him and trust Him and find strength through faith in His goodness.

Mordecai was one of the many Jews who had chosen to stay in Medo-Persia rather than return to Jerusalem. While it is true that fifty thousand went back with Zerubbabel, hundreds of thousands of others stayed behind. The Medes and Persians, under King Cyrus and King Darius, had been kind to them, letting them work and worship as they pleased, and it was easier to stay than to return. Some, like Mordecai and, later, Ezra and Nehemiah, found good jobs in the palace and became friends of the king. Others, scattered all over the country, got into one kind of business or another and took part in the life of the empire as though they belonged to it.

Exactly what Mordecai's duties were we are not told. The Bible says that he "sat in the king's gate," which may mean

132

he was an official in the court who, with other royal servants, waited near the palace entrance to obey the king's orders.

One evening, when Mordecai arrived home, he brought a most exciting story. There had been a lot of trouble in the palace. Queen Vashti had been deposed! At a wild drinking party the night before, King Xerxes (called Ahasuerus in the Bible) had ordered her to come to the party so that his chief princes could see her beauty—and she had refused. Yes, she had refused! She had actually disobeyed the king, an unheard-of thing in Persia, where a wife was supposed to do whatever she was told by her husband. In his anger Xerxes had said that Vashti was no longer queen. He wouldn't have her in the palace. She could go. And she had gone.

It was quite a story, and everybody was telling it to everybody else all over the empire.

I can hear little Esther saying, "But, dear Mordecai, what will they do for a queen? The king will have to have a queen, won't he?"

And Mordecai may well have said, "Yes, my dear, of course he will. He's probably looking for one now. Who knows? Perhaps he will want you to be his queen!"

"O no, he would never think of me," she said, laughing at her uncle's fun. "He'd never want a Jewish girl like me."

"You never can tell," said Mordecai. "Stranger things than that have happened. And what a lovely queen you would make, my little star!"

STORY 2

Orphan Girl Becomes Queen

THERE must have been a lot of excitement in Persia those days. Every girl from India to Ethiopia, in all the 127 provinces of the empire, was talking about the king's search for a new queen. Everyone hoped she would be the one to be chosen. And you may be sure that every mother was certain her daughter was the most worthy for this high honor.

By the king's command beauty contests—or the like—were held in every province, and the loveliest girls given a free trip to Shushan for the king's inspection.

As more and more girls arrived at the palace Mordecai had an idea. Why, his Esther was far more beautiful than any of these young ladies from Syria, Egypt, Arabia, and other parts of the country. They didn't stand a chance beside his precious little star. They weren't in the same class. Esther was far and away the best-looking girl in the world.

"I'm sure you could win," he told her one day, after seeing

some of the latest arrivals. "You're so much lovelier than any of the others. Why not try and see what happens? It could be that God wants you to be queen."

Finally Esther agreed, and Mordecai took her to "the king's house, to the custody of Hegai, keeper of the women."

As Mordecai bade her good-by he added one word of caution. "Don't tell anyone you are a Jewess," he said. "That might spoil everything."

"I won't," said Esther, and she was gone.

When Hegai saw Esther he was so struck with her beauty that he felt sure she would be chosen to be queen. So he gave her the best rooms in the house of the women and seven maidens to wait on her.

This was encouraging, but it didn't mean that Esther *would* be queen. After all, the king had to see all the other girls before he could make up his mind; and there might be someone else prettier than she.

As for poor Mordecai, he waited impatiently for news about his precious daughter. He felt certain that the king would choose her. How could he do otherwise? But suppose he didn't, what would happen to her? Would she be allowed to come home again?

"And Mordecai walked every day before the court of the women's house, to know how Esther did, and what should become of her."

Can't you see him pacing to and fro, looking up at the barred windows, hoping to get a glimpse of her face or a wave of her hand?

"O Esther, Esther, where are you?" I can hear him calling. "What has happened to you, my little star?"

Twelve months passed. Then one day Esther was called to meet the king. How excited she must have been! How hard she must have tried to look her very best! How she must have prayed for God's help and guidance on this greatest day of her life!

ORPHAN GIRL BECOMES QUEEN

Mordecai was waiting outside, you can be sure, and when Esther walked from the women's house to the throne room, dressed in the finest robes the Persian court could supply, and attended by all her lovely maidens, I can imagine he almost burst with pride. Such a dream she was, such a beautiful, glorious dream!

Onlookers in the corridors gasped in wonder as she passed by. Indeed she "found favour in the sight of all them that looked upon her."

At last she came into the "house royal" and the king was overcome by her breath-taking beauty. It was a case of love at first sight. "And the king loved Esther above all the women, and she obtained grace and favour in his sight more than all the virgins; so that he set the royal crown upon her head, and made her queen."

STORY 3

Plots in the Palace

NO KING was very safe on his throne in those days. Always there was somebody or another plotting to take his life.

The famous Xerxes was no exception. Soon after Esther became his queen two of his chamberlains, Bigthan and Teresh, became so angry at something he had done that they made up their minds to kill him.

Unfortunately for them, they talked about their plan to others, who whispered it to their friends, who whispered it to *their* friends, and so on, until finally the story reached Mordecai. He told Esther, and Esther told the king. The two plotters were arrested and put to death. But in all the excitement Mordecai was forgotten. The king did not even thank him for his help.

About this time Xerxes chose as his prime minister a man named Haman the Agagite—believed to have been a descendant of Agag, king of Amalek, whom the prophet Samuel slew.

It was not a good choice. He may have been strong, but

138

he was also proud, cruel, and ruthless. Mordecai did not like him and could not bring himself to bow to him as the law required.

When Haman came striding through the servants' quarters near the palace gate everybody paid him deep respect—everybody, that is, except Mordecai. He just looked the other way.

Day after day this went on, and soon all the king's servants were talking about it.

"You'll get into trouble," some of them said to Mordecai. "It's the king's orders that everybody bow to Haman. You'd better do it."

"Not I," said Mordecai. "I couldn't. Not to him."

And he didn't. Whereupon Haman became terribly angry. The sight of that one man standing erect when all the rest were bowing to him was more than he could endure.

About this time he learned that Mordecai was a Jew, and this gave him an idea. He would take his revenge not only on Mordecai, but on all the Jews. He would wipe them off the face of the earth.

To make quite sure that his plot would succeed he went to the priests of his heathen gods and had them cast lots to find the best time to purge the Jews from the Persian Empire. The lot fell upon the thirteenth day of the twelfth month.

Then he went to King Xerxes and outlined his plan, making out, of course, that he had thought of it in the best interests of king and country.

"There is a certain people scattered abroad and dispersed among the people in all the provinces of thy kingdom," he said; "and their laws are diverse from all people; neither keep they the king's laws: therefore it is not for the king's profit to suffer them. If it please the king, let it be written that they may be destroyed."

Lest the king object that so large an undertaking might cost too much money, he offered to pay all the expenses himself.

"I will pay ten thousand talents of silver to the hands of those that have charge of the business," he said.

So great was the king's confidence in Haman that he told him to do as he pleased. "Here, take my ring," he said; "write your own decree and sign it in my name."

Haman was delighted. Things were going better than he had dared to hope. He chuckled when he thought of what he would do to Mordecai in just a little while from now.

Calling the king's scribes, he had them prepare the decree, which was then sent to all the governors of the 127 provinces. It ordered them "to destroy, to kill, and to cause to perish, all Jews, both young and old, little children and women, in one day, even upon the thirteenth day of the twelfth month . . . and to take the spoil of them for a prey."

It was a terrible thing to do. It meant the massacre of the entire Jewish race. It was worse than anything Pharaoh had tried to do in Egypt. But what did Haman care? When the decree had been read in Shushan, he and the king "sat down to drink."

But they had forgotten something. They had failed to reckon with the God of Israel, who has a special care for His people. They had also overlooked the fact that He had a bright little star shining in the palace at that very moment.

141

STORY 4

Esther's Grand Decision

Y OU CAN imagine how Mordecai felt when he heard about the king's decree. The Bible says that he "rent his clothes, and put on sackcloth with ashes, and went out into the midst of the city, and cried with a loud and bitter cry."

All over Medo-Persia, wherever the decree was read, there were similar scenes of sorrow. In every city and village "there was great mourning among the Jews, and fasting, and weeping, and wailing; and many lay in sackcloth and ashes."

When Esther's maids told her how upset Mordecai was she wondered what could be the matter. Not knowing the cause, she sent him some new clothes to cheer him up, but he would not accept them. She guessed then that something serious must be wrong and sent her most trusted servant to find out what it was.

"Mordecai told him of all that had happened . . . , and of the sum of money that Haman had promised to pay to the

142

king's treasuries for the Jews, to destroy them. Also he gave him the copy of the writing of the decree . . . , to shew it unto Esther."

Mordecai begged Esther to go and see the king and persuade him to change his mind, but Esther sent back word to say she couldn't possibly do that. No one, not even the queen herself, was allowed to go to the king unless specially invited. It was a law, and death was the penalty for disobedience.

To this Mordecai replied, "Don't think you will escape" adding, in words that will live forever: "If thou altogether holdest thy peace at this time, then shall there enlargement and deliverance arise to the Jews from another place; but thou and thy father's house shall be destroyed: and *who knoweth whether thou art come to the kingdom for such a time as this?*"

Esther's heart was touched. Suddenly she understood why she, a little orphan girl, had been made queen. God had planned it! He knew this terrible crisis was coming and He had made her queen to save His people. She had indeed come to the kingdom for such a time as this.

But how could she go to the king? It was as much as her life was worth. Yet if God desired it, she would go, trusting in His protection.

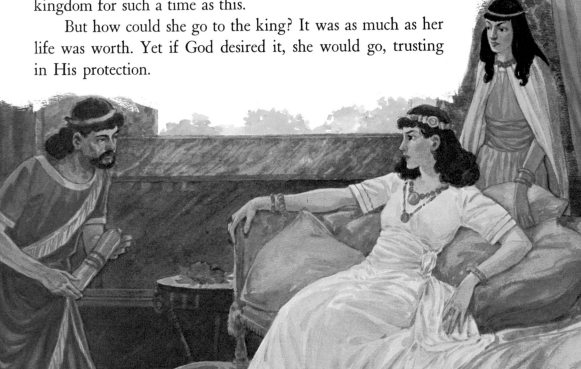

Back came the messenger to Mordecai with Esther's answer: "Go, gather together all the Jews that are present in Shushan, and fast ye for me, and neither eat nor drink three days, night or day: I also and my maidens will fast likewise; and so will I go in unto the king, which is not according to the law: and if I perish, I perish."

Brave Esther! Noble little star! What a grand decision she made!

How the Jews must have prayed for her during those next few days! Never had the synagogues of Shushan been so crowded with solemn-faced people, all pleading with God to watch over their dear, beautiful queen, and help her somehow to bring deliverance to her people.

In every Jewish home throughout the city boys and girls prayed also, for they knew full well that their lives were in danger too.

"Bless dear Queen Esther," I can hear them saying. "Keep her safe. Help her to be brave. Don't let any harm come to her. Make the king be nice to her. And don't let him kill us all."

So the prayers from young and old went heavenward, while angels drew near to help.

Meanwhile the face of God's little star shone brighter than ever as she plucked up her courage to go in to see the king.

STORY 5

Royal Invitation

ALL NEXT day, and the day after, Esther thought about what she should do. Suppose she should go to see the king, would he welcome her? And if so, what would she say to him? How could she possibly persuade him to change his mind and alter his decree? Persian kings never altered their decrees. It wasn't done.

Then too, Xerxes might be in a bad mood. He might be angry with her for coming to see him. He might have her put in prison, or executed. It was a terrible risk to take.

Then she had a bright idea. Calling her maids, she bade them prepare a very special banquet in her house. Then, putting on her royal robes, and looking more beautiful than ever, she made her way slowly to the king's house.

Presently she found herself at the entrance of the great hall where Xerxes was seated on his royal throne. Placing herself where he could see her, she wondered whether or not he would hold out his golden scepter as a token of welcome.

ROYAL INVITATION

He did. Catching sight of his lovely young queen, he smiled at her, bidding her come close to him.

As Esther touched the top of his golden scepter he asked what he could do for her. Graciously he offered to give her anything she wanted, even to half of his kingdom. Probably he didn't mean exactly that, but it sounded nice and was a custom in those days.

Esther was ready. She had made up her mind to make a very simple request at first—one that the king could hardly fail to grant. She would just invite him to dinner.

"If it seem good unto the king," she said very sweetly, "let the king and Haman come this day unto the banquet that I have prepared for him."

"Of course, of course!" said the king, no doubt relieved that she wanted so little of him and flattered at this mark of her approval of his prime minister. At once he sent a messenger to tell Haman to hurry up and do as the queen had asked.

Haman was overjoyed. This was the greatest reward he had ever received. To dine alone with the king and queen was an honor he had never dared to hope for.

That evening the two men came to Esther's apartment, where everything was beautifully prepared for them. They ate and drank happily together; then the king asked again, "What do you want, Esther? There must be something."

"There is," said Esther, with all her charm. "My request is that you will both come to dinner again tomorrow. Then I will tell you."

Gladly the king agreed; but his curiosity was yet more

147

— PAINTING BY HERBERT RUDEEN   © 1955, BY REVIEW AND HERALD

When the king held forth the golden scepter
to show that she was welcome in the court,
Queen Esther touched it, and asked the king
and Haman to be her guests at a royal dinner.

aroused. What could it be that the queen wanted? Clearly she had something important on her mind. What was it? He must find out.

As for Haman, he had never been so happy in his life. Hurrying home, he called his wife Zeresh and his closest friends and reported to them all that had happened. In his excitement he told of all "the glory of his riches" and how the king had promoted him above all his princes and servants.

"And now, to think of it," he added "the queen has invited me to dine with her and the king twice in two days! I'd be the happiest man in the world if it weren't for that Mordecai. He's the only man in the palace who refuses to bow when I pass by. He makes me so angry I can hardly contain myself."

ROYAL INVITATION

"Why bother about him?" said Zeresh. "Why let one old Jew spoil your happiness? Get him out of the way."

"Good idea!" said his friends. "Have a gallows made, the highest ever built in Shushan. Then when you meet the king to-morrow ask him to let you hang Mordecai on it. If he agrees, you can forget your troubles and go merrily to the banquet."

"And the thing pleased Haman; and he caused the gallows to be made."

Eighty-six feet high he made it—high enough so all the city could see his hated enemy dangling from it.

But he built it a little too soon.

STORY 6

The Biter Bitten

THAT night the king could not sleep. Maybe he was still thinking about Esther's banquet, or worrying about what was on her mind. Anyhow, sleep would not come. So he sent for the book of records and told a servant to read from it.

Now it so happened that the chapter the servant read was all about the two traitors, Bigthan and Teresh, who had tried to murder the king, and how Mordecai had discovered their plot just in time.

"What has been done for this man Mordecai?" asked the king.

"Nothing so far," said the servant.

At this moment who should enter the room but Haman, who had come to ask the king's permission to hang Mordecai.

Catching sight of him, the king said, "Haman, what shall be done to the man whom the king delights to honor?"

Thinking that the king must be planning some further

promotion for him, Haman replied, "Let him be dressed in the king's robes, with the royal crown on his head; and let him ride through the city on the king's horse, with one of the chief princes running before him crying, 'Thus shall it be done to the man whom the king delights to honor.'"

"Good," said the king. "Now do just that to Mordecai the Jew."

"Mordecai!" gasped Haman. "Not Mordecai!"

But he dared not disobey.

So the king's robes, the royal crown, and the royal horse were prepared as though Xerxes himself were going to use them. Then Mordecai was dressed up as the King of Persia.

Surely he must have been the most surprised man in Shushan that day. And how all the princes and the servants

and even the king himself must have laughed as they saw Haman start running ahead of Mordecai through the palace gates crying, "Thus shall it be done to the man whom the king delights to honor!"

As the strange procession passed along the city streets thousands of men and women, boys and girls, gaped in wonder.

"Surely it can't be Haman," I can hear them saying. "Not the prime minister himself, running before Mordecai the Jew!"

Before nightfall all Shushan must have been rocking with laughter.

No doubt Mordecai was amused, too; but as for Haman, it was more than he could take. Hurrying home, he poured out his tale of woe to Zeresh. Never had he been so crushed.

He must have been tired, too, after so long a run, but he had no time to rest. For even while he was talking, the king's chamberlains arrived to lead him in state to Esther's banquet.

How he had looked forward to this occasion! Now he didn't care whether he went or not. Would the king tease him about what had happened that afternoon? What would the queen say, if she had heard of it? And now how could he ask the king to hang Mordecai?

The banquet began. Richly dressed servants waited on the king and queen and Haman. The most delicate foods which the palace cooks could provide were spread on the table.

By and by the king, unable to wait longer to satisfy his curiosity, asked, "What is your petition, Esther? What do you want of me?"

152

"I ask my life and the life of my people," she said boldly, but pleadingly. "For we are sold, I and my people, to be destroyed, to be slain, and to perish."

"Who is there in my kingdom who would dare to think of such a thing?" asked the king in great surprise.

"Haman," said the queen. "This wicked Haman."

White with anger, the king rose from his seat and strode out into the palace garden, leaving Haman alone with the queen.

Sensing his danger, Haman began to plead for Esther's forgiveness. He wanted her to beg the king not to have him put to death. In a frenzy of fear he flung himself on the couch where she was resting.

At that moment the king returned. Now he became more furious than ever. Thinking Haman planned some

153

harm to the queen he called upon his servants to arrest him at once.

As they dragged Haman out of the banqueting room someone asked what was to be done with him.

Pointing out of the window, one of the chamberlains said, "Behold the gallows which Haman made for Mordecai."

"Hang him thereon!" cried the king.

"So they hanged Haman on the gallows that he had prepared for Mordecai."

Such was the fate of the man who plotted to kill all the children of Israel in one day.

And thus was the biter bitten.

STORY 7

Day of Victory

WITH the death of Haman a great change came over the Persian court. Mordecai was made prime minister, and all Haman's property was given to Queen Esther, who appointed Mordecai its guardian.

However, the death of Haman did not remove the threat to the Jews. The king's decree still stood, and could not be changed. Unless something unusual should happen the entire Hebrew race—including those who had returned to Jerusalem—would be put to death on the thirteenth day of the twelfth month.

Esther decided to see the king about it again. As before, he held out his golden scepter in welcome to her, but this time, instead of inviting him to dinner, she fell on her knees before him and with tears begged him to save her people.

"How can I endure to see the evil that shall come unto my people?" she cried, "or how can I endure to see the destruction of my kindred?"

With a Jewess as his queen and a Jew as his prime minister, the king was in a very difficult place. He saw at once that something must be done. But he did not know what to do. So he told Esther that she could write her own decree and seal it with the king's ring and send it out to all the governors of the provinces, provided only that she did not reverse what he had written before.

This rolled the problem of how to save the Jews back on Esther and Mordecai. So the two got together and tried to think of a way out. They no doubt prayed hard for God to show them what to do.

They came up with a very bright idea. In the king's name they would tell the Jews to defend themselves from attack on the thirteenth day of the twelfth month.

So they drew up a document commanding the Jews to "gather themselves together, and to stand for their life, to de-

stroy, to slay, and to cause to perish, all the power of the people and province that would assault them, both little ones and women."

When the decree was written, Mordecai sealed it with the king's ring and addressed it "to the lieutenants, and the deputies and rulers of the provinces which are from India unto Ethiopia." Then he sent it by "posts on horseback, and riders on mules, camels, and young dromedaries."

The whole Persian postal system went into action. And what a wonderful scene it must have been as riders on all those different animals rode out of Shushan bearing the message that was to save God's people!

There was no slackness either, for "the posts that rode upon mules and camels went out, being hastened and pressed on by the king's commandment."

It took many weeks for the decree to reach all the distant provinces of the empire, but it arrived in time. And as the Jews read it, they were greatly relieved. "In every province, and in every city, whithersoever the king's commandment and his decree came, the Jews had joy and gladness, a feast and a good day. And many of the people of the land became Jews; for the fear of the Jews fell upon them."

Then came the thirteenth day of the twelfth month. On this day, by the king's first decree, the people of the land had the right to kill all Jews and take their property; but few acted on it. Where they did, they found the Jews ready for them. The result was that the day many feared would be a day of destruction became a day of victory.

And so once more, in His wonderful way, God guarded His people and saved them from the harm that wicked men plotted against them. Again the Seed of the woman was preserved from the hatred of the serpent; and God's loving purpose for man's redemption moved one step nearer to its final triumph.

PART IV

Stories of Famous Men

(JOB, JONAH, JOEL, MALACHI)

STORY 1

Man With Ten Children

LONG, long ago—long before Esther was born, or Solomon, or even Joshua—there lived a man "in the land of Uz, whose name was Job."

This man had ten children—seven boys and three girls. I wish I knew their names but the Bible doesn't tell them.

Just where Job lived nobody knows for sure. Many think that the land of Uz must have been somewhere on the border of Arabia, because it was a fertile land near a great wilderness.

Job was a very rich man and was known as "the greatest of all the men of the east." He owned seven thousand sheep, five hundred yoke of oxen, and five hundred she asses. What a wonderful time his ten children must have had with all those animals!

But though Job was rich and had "a very great household" he was not a worldly man. He did not let his money turn his head. He put God first in everything and became known as a "perfect and upright" man who loved God and hated evil.

6-11

161

Before God permitted Satan to try Job's integrity, the patriarch was one of the wealthiest men in ancient times. Yet he was faithful to God and happy with his ten children.

What a good example he must have set before his children, his friends, and neighbors! Surely his noble character was his greatest wealth!

When God wanted to name three righteous men, whom do you suppose He chose? The prophet Ezekiel tells us. They were Noah, Daniel, and Job. This was the greatest tribute He could pay to any man. Wouldn't you like to be on God's list too?

With his large family of boys and girls, with all his sheep and camels and oxen, and, best of all, with the feeling that God's smile was upon him, Job must have been a very happy man.

Just imagine all those boys and girls running through the house! Can't you see them playing all sorts of tricks, laughing and shrieking for joy as children will? I am sure Job picked them up when they fell, loved them when they got hurt, prayed with them when they were naughty, and led them ever heavenward by his godly life. Those were good, glad days.

As the years rolled by and the children grew up, the boys set up homes of their own; but the family remained unbroken and the ten brothers and sisters still had a wonderful time together. First one, then another, would have a party in his house and invite all the rest; and you can be sure they often

talked of their childhood pranks and their dear father and mother who, they knew, were still praying for them as of old.

All this happiness was too great, perhaps, to last. Of a sudden it began to fade away.

One day a messenger came rushing up to Job in great excitement. "The oxen were plowing," he gasped, "and the asses feeding beside them: and the Sabeans fell upon them, and took them away; yea, they have slain the servants with the edge of the sword; and I only am escaped."

"Cattle thieves," muttered Job, wondering how many of his animals had been stolen. He would have to do something about this.

But scarcely had the first messenger finished his story when another arrived, fear showing on his face. "The fire of God is fallen from heaven," he cried, "and . . . burned up the sheep, and the servants, and consumed them; and I only am escaped."

So! What a storm it must have been! What fearful lightning! How sad that so many of the shepherds should have been killed!

At that moment a third messenger came running with still worse news. The Chaldeans, he said, had come in three bands and driven off all the camels.

This was the greatest loss so far. Camels were valuable beasts and to lose so many at once was a heavy blow. Coming on top of everything else it was enough to shake anyone: but Job could stand it, so long as his children were unharmed. "God grant nothing happens to them," I can hear him praying.

But then it came, the most terrible news of all. His eldest son had invited his brothers and sisters to a party in his house. They were all together—so happy, so carefree—when "a great wind from the wilderness" struck the house with the fury of a tornado, smashing it to pieces and killing everyone inside.

This was too much. Job didn't mind so much about losing his oxen and asses, his sheep and camels, but his children! This was heartbreaking!

Tearing his clothes and shaving his head—as was the custom in those days when great sorrows came—"he fell down upon the ground, and worshipped."

"Naked came I into the world," he mourned, "and naked shall I leave it."

Humbly, sadly, he cried, "The Lord gave, and the Lord hath taken away; blessed be the name of the Lord."

"In all this Job sinned not, nor charged God foolishly."

No wonder God loved him and counted him among the three best men who ever lived!

STORY 2

What Job Didn't Know

POOR Job! How he must have wondered why all these terrible things had happened to him! Was God punishing him for something he had done wrong?

Why had he lost everything all at once? Why had the Sabaeans stolen his oxen and asses? Why had the lightning struck his sheep? Why had the Chaldeans driven off his camels? Why had God allowed his children to be killed by the windstorm? Why had not one of them at least been spared?

Oh, why, why, why? It must have been so hard to understand, especially when he had tried his very best to be true and faithful to God.

If only he could have known all we know today! But he didn't. He was left to wonder and wonder and question and question, with nobody to give him an answer.

Whoever wrote the book of Job—and many believe it was Moses—has drawn back the curtain and let us see why so much trouble came to Job all at once.

165

It was Satan who was back of it all—the very same person who got Adam and Eve to question and disobey God in the Garden of Eden.

One day, so the story goes, "when the sons of God came to present themselves before the Lord," Satan turned up too.

"Where have you come from?" asked the Lord.

"From going to and fro in the earth," said Satan, "and from walking up and down in it."

"Did you meet Job?" asked the Lord. "There's no one like him in all the earth. Perfect and upright, he loves Me and hates evil."

"Does Job serve God for nought?" sneered Satan. "He's good because he's rich. You have blessed him and protected him and given him everything a man could wish for. No wonder he serves You! Take away all he has and he will curse You to Your face."

God would not believe it. He trusted Job. He felt sure that whether Job had much or little he would still be true to Him.

"Try and see," the Lord told Satan, "only don't hurt him."

Satan left in great glee, eagerly planning the evil he would bring on Job. And soon the blows began to fall, one after another, while all heaven watched to see what Job would do.

Job never wavered. True, he couldn't understand why God had allowed such trials to come to him, but he trusted God's goodness just the same.

You may be sure God was proud of Job. What a man was this, suffering so much without a murmur!

As for Satan, he was furious, for although he had tried

166

his very best to shake Job's faith, he had failed miserably.

When next he met the Lord he excused his failure by saying that he hadn't had a fair chance.

"You see Job still holds fast his integrity," the Lord said to him.

"Only because You would not let me touch his person," sneered Satan. "All that a man has will he give for his life. Touch his bone and his flesh and he will curse You to Your face."

"All right," agreed the Lord, still sure that Job would keep true to Him. "He is in your hands. Only save his life."

So Satan went forth "from the presence of the Lord, and smote Job with sore boils from the sole of his foot unto his crown."

The big test was on. How would Job come out of it?

Unknown to him, both God and Satan—and no doubt thousands upon thousands of angels—watched intently to see what he would do now.

All Job knew was that the boils were very painful. With the wretched things all over him, he could neither sit, stand, nor lie in comfort. They itched, they ached, they hurt, and there was nothing he could do for them except scrape the pus away with a piece of broken crockery.

Week after week the torture went on. How long were the days! How endless the nights! And still there was no relief.

Coming on top of all his losses and the death of all his children it was enough to break any man's spirit.

"Curse God and die," urged his wife, who was greatly upset by all that had happened. No doubt she was still weeping over the sudden death of all her boys and girls she had loved so dearly. And now Job was so ill, and looked so terrible, that she wanted him to get it over with. Better give up trying to be good. It wasn't worth while.

But Job was still unmoved.

"You speak as one of the foolish women," he said to her. "What? shall we receive good at the hand of God, and shall we not receive evil?"

In other words, shall we not trust God in bad times as well as in good? Shall we give up our faith just because things go wrong?

"In all this did not Job sin with his lips."

How pleased God must have been with him!

And what a lesson Job's faithfulness has for us! When trouble comes it is so easy to say, "God doesn't love me any more; He has turned against me." But we must never say that. God loves us always—forever and ever. Should trials come to us they will come as a test of our love for Him.

Let us make up our minds that we will be faithful and true whatever happens—in sunshine or rain, in good times or bad.

STORY 3

Tried and True

S NEWS spread about the troubles that had come to Job, tongues started wagging all over the place.

Many found the story hard to believe, for Job had been such a rich man and so highly respected by everybody. If he was indeed suffering as much as was reported, then there must be a reason. Surely he must have done something very wicked and God was punishing him for it.

From far and near his friends came to see him, and they were shocked by what they saw. Indeed, Job was so changed that they hardly recognized him.

Three of his friends were Eliphaz the Temanite, Bildad the Shuhite, and Zophar the Naamathite. When they saw him they were so upset that they tore their clothes and sprinkled dust on their heads. Then "they sat down with him upon the ground seven days and seven nights, and none spake a word unto him: for they saw that his grief was very great."

What a week that was! As the hours passed slowly by

169

not a sound was heard but the groans of the sick man.

When at last Job spoke it was to say, "I wish I had never been born!" How he suffered!

"Why didn't I die at my birth?" he cried. "For now should I have lain still and been quiet, I should have slept: then had I been at rest. . . . There the wicked cease from troubling; and there the weary be at rest."

Rest! That was all he wanted now. Rest from his troubles; rest from his suffering! If only the pain would stop and he could sleep! He even wished that he could die.

Then his three friends began to talk, but they did not bring him much comfort. They were sure he must be a very great sinner, and they begged him to make things right with God.

"Happy is the man whom God corrects," said Eliphaz; "therefore despise not the chastening of the Almighty."

Bildad said that maybe all this trouble had come because Job's children had sinned. He, too, was certain that suffering was a sign that God had been offended. "God will not cast away a perfect man," he said, "neither will He help the evil doers." It never occurred to him, or to any of the other friends, that this suffering might be a test of Job's faith, or that Satan, not God, was the cause of all the evil that had come to him.

Meanwhile Job continued to declare his innocence. Once,

170

addressing God, he said, "Thou knowest that I am not wicked." Then to his friends he boldly declared, "Though he slay me, yet will I trust in him."

"My friends scorn me," he cried: "but mine eye poureth out tears unto God."

No, he would not give up his faith in God's love and goodness. "The righteous also shall hold on his way," he said, "and he that hath clean hands shall be stronger and stronger."

How brave of him to speak like this when he felt so weak!

Oh, yes, he still wondered why it had all happened. Often he thought about the days when he had been rich and powerful and respected, "when the Almighty was yet with me, when my children were about me; when I washed my steps with butter, and the rock poured me out rivers of oil; when . . . the young men saw me, and hid themselves: and the aged arose, and stood up."

Now it seemed to him that God, for some reason, had forsaken him. He has "stripped me of my glory, and taken the crown from my head," he said. He has "destroyed me on every side, and I am gone" and He counts me "as one of his enemies." But even so he loved God still and was sure someday all would come out right.

"I know that my redeemer liveth," he told his friends, "and that he shall stand at the latter day upon the earth: and though after my skin worms destroy this body, yet in my flesh shall I see God: whom I shall see for myself and not another."

Marvelous faith! You would think his three friends would have agreed that he must be right. But no. Back came Eliphaz with the same old charge, "Is not your wickedness great?" Then he taunted the poor sick man by saying, "Is it any pleasure to the Almighty that you are righteous? Or is it gain to Him that you make your way perfect?" "Return to the Almighty," he urged, and "put away iniquity."

"I have not gone back from the commandment of His lips," retorted Job. "I have esteemed the words of His mouth more than my necessary food." "He knows the way that I take: when He has tried me, I shall come forth as gold."

In a wonderful defense of his way of life and of his striving to do the will of God the best he knew how, he said:

"If I have walked with vanity . . .

"If any blot has cleaved to my hands . . .

"If I did despise the cause of my manservant . . .

"If I have made gold my hope . . .

"If I rejoiced because my wealth was great . . .

"If I rejoiced at the destruction of him that hated me . . .

"If I covered my transgressions . . . " then "let me be weighed in an even balance, that God may know my integrity." If he had done wrong it was not on purpose, and he was sure God was too just to punish him unfairly.

Remember, this all happened thousands of years ago. Job had no Bible to guide him, for no part of it had been written. There was no church pastor to visit him and cheer his heart, for the church did not exist as we know it today. He stood alone for God and the right. What faith! What courage! No wonder God reckoned him among His most loyal and noble champions.

STORY 4

All's Well That Ends Well

WHEN Job's friends had finished talking, God broke in.

"The Lord answered Job out of the whirlwind," and what He said makes one of the most wonderful chapters in all the Bible—Job 38. You must read it all through someday.

God asked Job many questions that he could not answer, such as, "Where were you when I laid the foundations of the earth, when the morning stars sang together and all the sons of God shouted for joy?"

"Who shut up the sea with doors . . . and said, Hitherto shalt thou come, but no further: and here shall thy proud waves be stayed?"

"Have you considered the treasures of the snow or the hail?" God asked. "Where does ice come from, and the hoarfrost?"

"Can you 'bind the sweet influences of the Pleiades, or loose the bands of Orion? or . . . guide Arcturus with his sons?' "

"Who provides food for the ravens? Did you give 'goodly wings unto the peacocks? or wings and feathers unto the ostrich?' Does the hawk fly by your wisdom? Does the eagle mount up at your command?"

As God continued to talk of the wonders of His creation Job became more and more aware of his own weakness.

He saw that, though he had tried hard to do God's will and live a holy life, he was still just a poor sinner in the presence of Him who made the heavens and the earth.

"I know that thou canst do every thing," he cried, "and that no thought can be withholden from thee. . . . I have heard of thee by the hearing of the ear: but now mine eye seeth thee. Wherefore I abhor myself, and repent in dust and ashes." "I am vile; what shall I answer thee? I will lay mine hand upon my mouth."

ALL'S WELL THAT ENDS WELL

God had loved Job all along, but now He loved him even more for his humility.

To Eliphaz, God said, "I am angry with you and your two friends, for you have not spoken right as has my servant Job." Then He told them to take seven bullocks and seven rams and offer them up as a burnt offering. "My servant Job will pray for you," He added.

This was the turning point in Job's long and terrible suffering. When the three friends brought the animals and offered them as a sacrifice, Job prayed for them.

"And the Lord turned the captivity of Job, when he prayed for his friends."

A new day now dawned for this faithful servant of Jehovah. His boils disappeared. His health and strength returned. More and more he felt—and looked—like his old self.

Brothers, sisters, friends, began to visit him again. They even took up a collection to give him a new start in life. "Every man also gave him a piece of money, and every one an earring of gold."

It was very kind of them, but they need not have troubled themselves, for God had big plans in mind for this dear man. Indeed "the Lord blessed the latter end of Job more than his

beginning." In just a little while Job had fourteen thousand sheep, six thousand camels, one thousand yoke of oxen, and one thousand she asses.

So "the Lord gave Job twice as much as he had before."

Best of all, God gave him ten more children, seven boys and three girls, just the same number as he had lost in that dreadful windstorm.

For some reason we have not been told the names of these seven boys. But we do know the names of the three girls. They are Jemima, Kezia, and Kerenhappuch.

"And in all the land were no women found so fair as the daughters of Job."

Maybe you are wondering how anyone could have so many children twice in one lifetime? Well, remember that Job was one of the ancient patriarchs who lived a long, long time. The Bible says that after his great trial and suffering, he lived 140 years "and saw his sons, and his son's sons, even four generations."

So everything turned out right in the end. What happened to the three friends Eliphaz, Bildad, and Zophar, we are not told. As to how Satan felt when he saw his wicked plans come to nought nothing is said. But we do know that "the patience of Job," his unfailing loyalty and love, will be remembered forever.

STORY 5

Swallowed by a Fish

ONE of the most exciting stories in the Bible is that of the man who was swallowed by a fish.

It happened a little more than a hundred years after the death of Solomon, when Palestine was divided between the kingdom of Judah and the kingdom of Israel, and Assyria ruled the world.

At that time "the word of the Lord came unto Jonah . . . saying, Arise, go to Nineveh, that great city, and cry against it."

Nineveh was the capital of Assyria, known everywhere for its wickedness and cruelty. It was the last place to which Jonah wanted to go. Had God asked him to go to Jerusalem, or Samaria, or even Damascus, he would no doubt have gone gladly; but Nineveh! Oh, no! Not Nineveh! There was no knowing what the people would do to a preacher of righteousness there.

So Jonah made up his mind to go as far from Nineveh as he could, to some place where God could not find him.

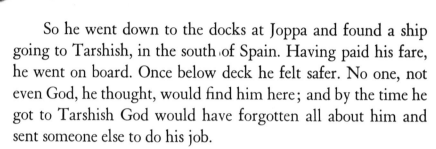

So he went down to the docks at Joppa and found a ship going to Tarshish, in the south of Spain. Having paid his fare, he went on board. Once below deck he felt safer. No one, not even God, he thought, would find him here; and by the time he got to Tarshish God would have forgotten all about him and sent someone else to do his job.

But he never got to Tarshish.

Nobody can run away from God; and when the ship weighed anchor and made for the harbor mouth He was closer to Jonah than ever.

Weary and discouraged, Jonah soon fell fast asleep. But God didn't. He had His eyes on that ship and His runaway prophet.

Pretty soon the wind began to rise. The choppy sea became rougher and rougher, tossing the tiny vessel about like a cork. Great waves began to break over her bow, and both captain and crew feared she would founder.

As the tempest grew worse they threw the cargo overboard. Then, with the ship rolling this way and that in what seemed to be her last agonies, every man began to cry to his god for help. Some cried to Baal, some to Ashtoreth, some to Moloch: but no help came. At that moment the captain, going below

178

perhaps to see if the ship had sprung a leak, found Jonah asleep. Angrily awaking him, he cried roughly:

"What do you mean, O sleeper? arise, call upon your God!"

Jonah staggered to his feet in a daze. But the awful pitching and tossing told him that the captain was right. The ship and all on board were in deadly danger.

As he joined the crew some of them said, "Let's cast lots and find out who brought this evil upon us." This they did, "and the lot fell upon Jonah."

Then they all turned upon the runaway prophet with one question after another. "What is your occupation?" they asked. "Where do you come from?" "What is your nationality?" "Why are you traveling on this ship?"

"I am a Hebrew," said Jonah, "and I fear the Lord, the God of heaven, who has made the sea and the dry land."

Then he told how God had called him to preach in Nineveh and how he was afraid, and ran off in the opposite direction.

"What shall we do . . . that the sea may be calm?" they asked anxiously.

"Throw me overboard," said Jonah.

But the men didn't want to do that. It seemed too cruel. So they bent to the oars again and rowed their hardest to bring the ship to land.

It was no use. The waves were too much for them. They had to give up. Then they came to Jonah again. Was he still willing to be thrown overboard? He was. He knew in his heart that all this trouble had come because of his disobedience. And why should so many die because of his sin?

"So they took up Jonah, and cast him forth into the sea."

Almost immediately the wind died and the sea became calm.

As for poor Jonah, he went down, down, down into the dark green water, certain that he was about to drown. Then of a sudden he had the strange feeling of being sucked down a slippery tube. No longer was he fighting for breath in the ocean, but trying hard not to breathe the foul air of some great beast's stomach.

He had been swallowed by a fish!

No, it is not impossible. Men have

been swallowed by whales since then, and lived to tell the tale. And remember that the Bible doesn't say that it was a whale that swallowed Jonah, but "a great fish" that God had prepared for this purpose.

Anyway, poor Jonah was inside the fish and he stayed there for "three days and three nights" which, to the Hebrews of those times, meant parts of three days.

For a while at least he was conscious, for he prayed for help from the fish's belly. What a prayer that must have been. What a confession of sin! What a cry for forgiveness! Wouldn't you pray very hard if you found yourself in such a dreadful place?

Telling God about his ordeal afterward, Jonah said, "The floods compassed me about: all thy billows and thy waves passed over me. Then I said, I am cast out of thy sight; yet I will look again toward thy holy temple.

"The waters compassed me about, even to the soul: the depth closed me round about, the weeds [eaten by the fish] were wrapped about my head. I went down to the bottoms of the mountains. . . .

"When my soul fainted within me I remembered the Lord: and my prayer came in unto thee, into thine holy temple. . . . Salvation is of the Lord."

In some wonderful way God spoke to the fish "and it vomited out Jonah upon the dry land."

PAINTING BY WILLIAM HUTCHINSON

What a frightening experience it was for poor Jonah. How terribly dark and hot and slimy it must have been in the stomach of the fish. It was like being buried alive, and we can imagine that Jonah's hair may have turned white with shock.

You may be sure the people of Nineveh listened to the prophet for he had a most solemn story to tell.

Here was a man whose life God had spared in a most marvelous way. His message must be from heaven. So when he cried, "Yet forty days, and Nineveh shall be overthrown," the people believed him and repented of their sins "from the greatest of them even to the least of them." Even the king himself put off his royal robes, "covered him with sackcloth, and sat in ashes," and published a decree saying, "Let man and beast be covered with sackcloth, and cry mightily unto God: yea, let them turn every one from his evil way, and from the violence that is in their hands."

What a revival! What a turning back to God! Never had there been such preaching; never such wonderful results.

All Nineveh—wicked Nineveh—had repented! And to think that Jonah had tried his best to run away from the job! What a lesson to all of us to do what God asks of us, then and there!

STORY 6

Gourd That Died Overnight

YOU would think that Jonah would have rejoiced at the wonderful results of his preaching, but he didn't. Oh, at first he did, no doubt, but when the forty days passed and the city wasn't destroyed, he became angry. He was afraid the people would call him a false prophet.

Gloomily he walked some distance out of the city, built a little booth to shield himself from the sun, and sat down to see what would happen next. Perhaps God would yet destroy the city after all; and if some fiery doom was going to descend from heaven he wanted to see it.

Just then the tiny seed of a gourd, or vine, began to grow beside Jonah. At first he did not notice it, but soon, as vines will, it spread all over his little booth, making him much cooler.

But it didn't last long. Next morning the vine was dead. A worm had cut its stem, causing it to wither. Then a wind came up and blew it away, leaving Jonah exposed to the hot sun. Now he became more angry still, thinking of how un-

183

comfortable he was. He felt out of sorts with everything.

"Do you do well to be angry with the gourd?" God asked him.

"Yes," snapped Jonah, quite impatiently.

Said God, "You have pity on the gourd which came up in a night and perished in a night: should not I spare Nineveh, that great city, wherein are more than 120,000 people?"

What a lesson in forgiveness! Jonah was thinking about himself, his comfort, and his reputation as a prophet; but God was thinking of all the thousands of people in the city. Had they not just repented of their sins? Were they not even now sitting in sackcloth and ashes? How then could He punish them? Was it not far better to pardon than to destroy them?

Long years afterward, when Christ's disciples wanted to call fire down from heaven to destroy a village that would not receive Him, Jesus said, "The Son of man is not come to destroy men's lives, but to save them."

God is ever the same—"merciful, slow to anger, and of great kindness." He is a God of compassion and tender love, ready to forgive the worst prodigal the moment he is sorry for his sins. May He put the same sweet spirit in our hearts and make us more like Him!

STORY 7

Great Things for God

NOT many years after Jonah preached to the people of Nineveh a man with a similar name took almost the same message to the people of Judah.

This man was Joel, and God sent him to Jerusalem to declare, "The day of the Lord is at hand!"

"Blow . . . the trumpet in Zion," he cried, "and sound an alarm in my holy mountain: let all the inhabitants of the land tremble: for the day of the Lord cometh, for it is nigh at hand."

Joel did not set a time for the coming judgment, but he did beg the people to repent. In God's name he pleaded, "Turn . . . to me with all your heart, and with fasting, and with weeping, and with mourning: and rend your heart, and not your garments, and turn unto the Lord your God: for he is gracious and merciful, slow to anger, and of great kindness."

Here again was the beautiful message of God's forgiving love. Repentance would bring instant pardon. Their punishment would be forgotten if only they would say, "I'm sorry."

185

But they must be sincere. To this end Joel begged them to get together and pray to God. "Gather the people," he urged, "assemble the elders, gather the children"—even the babes in arms. Let everybody cry, "Spare thy people, O Lord!"

All sorts of good things would come to them if only they would give themselves to God like this. He was just waiting to be gracious to them.

There was no need to be afraid. "Fear not, O land," he cried; "be glad and rejoice: for the Lord will do great things."

Great things! Yes, indeed. God was ready to pour out His Holy Spirit upon them. Even the boys and girls would prophesy, the old men dream dreams, and the young men see visions. There would be no limit to the great things they would all dream about and do by God's grace. For all His faithful ones He would show wonders in heaven and on earth and His saving power would be seen in a wonderful way in Jerusalem.

It was a marvelous promise, and the pity is that the people took no notice of it. Because they would not give up their sins they cut themselves off from all the good God planned for them. The great things He had in mind for them never happened. Jerusalem was destroyed and the people taken into captivity.

But the promise still stands. It is there in the Bible for anyone who wants to claim it. It is there for every boy and girl in the whole wide world.

GREAT THINGS FOR GOD

All you have to do to receive it is to turn to the Lord *with all your heart*. From that moment He will begin to pour out His Spirit upon you. He will cause you to dream dreams and see visions of the great things that He wants done today. Then He will help you to make those dreams come true.

Have you ever stopped to think how many great things God wants to do today through boys and girls like you?

There is so much trouble in the world, so much fear and strife, that He is looking for great peacemakers—men of courage, wisdom, and patience, who will stand between enemies, between people of different nations and races, and draw them together with cords of love.

There is so much sickness in the world, so much suffering and sadness, that He is looking for great healers—men of skill and kindness who will minister to the sick of mind and body.

There is so much sin in the world, and so much sadness resulting from it, that He is looking for great preachers—men "mighty in the scriptures" who will declare His love with boldness and turn many from their evil ways.

Would you do great things for God? Would you be a great missionary, a great teacher, a great leader of youth, a great builder of Christ's church on earth?

You may. Dream glorious dreams. Plan with wide and glowing vision. Don't be afraid. "Be glad and rejoice: for the Lord will do great things"—for you!

STORY 8

Heaven's Windows

DOES heaven really have windows? The Bible says so. But, of course, it doesn't mean glass windows that open sideways or push up and down.

"Windows of heaven" is really just another word picture telling of God's love and His willingness to do great and wonderful things for all who serve Him faithfully.

In olden times it was a custom on feast days, weddings, and other celebrations for rich people to open the upper windows of their homes and throw gold and silver coins to passers-by below. This may have led the prophet to say that God would open "the windows of heaven, and pour you out a blessing." "Empty out" a blessing, the margin reads, and that makes the picture clearer still.

Malachi wrote the last book of the Old Testament and, like all the other books, it is an appeal to people to live so that God can bless them. God wants to bless everybody. His greatest joy is to see men and women happy. Always He stands ready

189

PAINTING BY HERBERT RUDEEN   © 1955, BY REVIEW AND HERALD

st as the rich people in olden times threw
oney to the poor at weddings and on feast
ys, so God promises to open heaven's win-
ws and pour out His blessings on tithers.

to pour His blessings upon them. But He can only do it for those who obey Him and do what's right and good.

One big trouble with the people in Malachi's day—about fifty years after Nehemiah was governor of Jerusalem—was that they would not pay the tithe that God had said was to be used to support the priests and Levites.

You may remember that when Nehemiah began his reforms, he had the people promise that they would not only keep the Sabbath faithfully but also pay tithe again as their fathers had done of old. But the promise was forgotten, and by the time Malachi came on the scene they had been doing wrong so long they thought it was right.

They were full of arguments to prove there was nothing the matter with what they were doing. When Malachi said that they had made God weary with their words they answered, "Wherein have we wearied him?"

When he pleaded with them to return to God, they said, "Wherein shall we return?"

When he accused them of robbing God they replied, "Wherein have we robbed thee?"

"I'll tell you," said Malachi, and he did. He told them they had robbed God by keeping back their tithes and offerings. This money did not belong to them, but to God. When they used it for themselves they were stealing. They were no better than thieves and robbers, no matter how good they thought they were.

"You are cursed with a curse," he went on: "For you have robbed me, even this whole nation."

190

Then, still speaking for God, he begged them to be obedient and make it possible for them to receive the blessings God waited to give them.

"Bring . . . all the tithes into the storehouse, that there may be meat in mine house, and prove me now herewith, saith the Lord of hosts, if I will not *open you the windows of heaven,* and pour you out a blessing, that there shall not be room enough to receive it."

Nor was this all. Other blessings would follow. God would watch over their land, their trees, their crops, their vineyards. He would even keep the insects from damaging them.

"I will rebuke the devourer for your sakes, and he shall not destroy the fruits of your ground; neither shall your vine cast her fruit before the time in the field, saith the Lord of hosts.

"And all nations shall call you blessed."

This is another of God's gracious promises that all may claim today. And what a lovely thought it is that any boy or girl can open the windows of heaven any time he wishes! The way is plain. All one has to do is to pay God a faithful tithe—one tenth of one's "increase"—in a spirit of love and devotion.

That may mean one tenth of ten cents earned by raking leaves for a neighbor, or one tenth of a dollar gained by selling a bicycle or a fishing rod. The amount you earn doesn't matter. It's the spirit that counts—the purpose to put God first in your thoughts and in your love.

Just do that and the windows of heaven will open and blessings more wonderful than you ever dreamed of will come tumbling down upon you.

In Malachi's day most of the people wouldn't believe what he said, but some did. They talked about it, saying, "We'll do what God has asked of us. We'll trust Him to keep His promises."

And then a remarkable thing happened. The Lord heard what they said to each other, for they said it over and over again. "And a book of remembrance was written before him for them that feared the Lord, and that thought upon his name."

"And they shall be mine," said the Lord, "in that day when I make up my special treasure."

How very wonderful! The people who love Him, and think of Him, and talk of Him, and give of their treasure to help His work—they shall be *His* treasure, His *"special treasure."* Yes, says God, and "I will spare them, as a man spares his own son who serves him." Nothing will be too good for Him to give them.

Would you like to have your name written in God's book of remembrance? Would you like to be His *"special treasure"*? You may if you will. Just tell Him so now.